Rick and Morty

VOLUME ONE

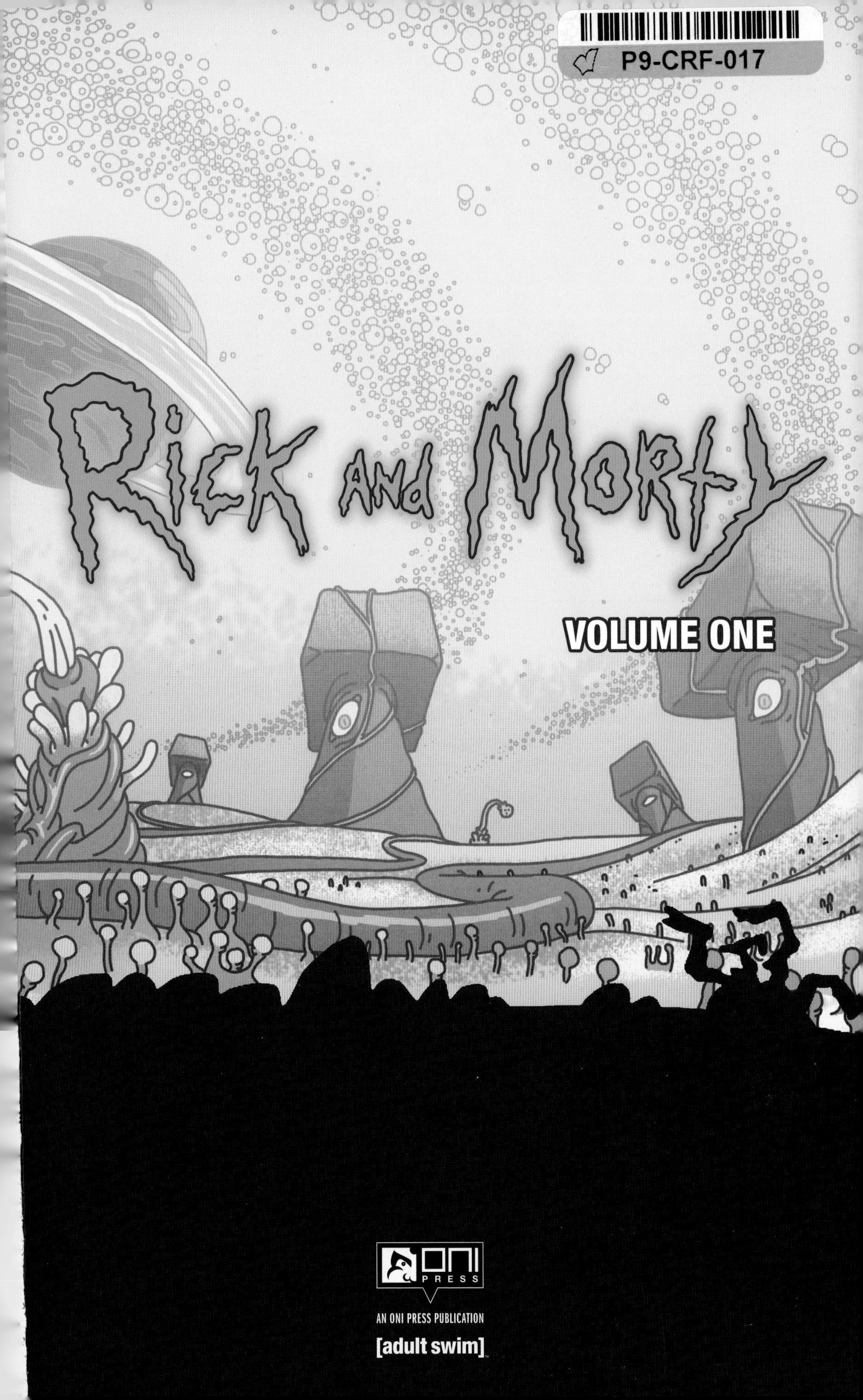

ONI PRESS

AN ONI PRESS PUBLICATION

[adult swim]

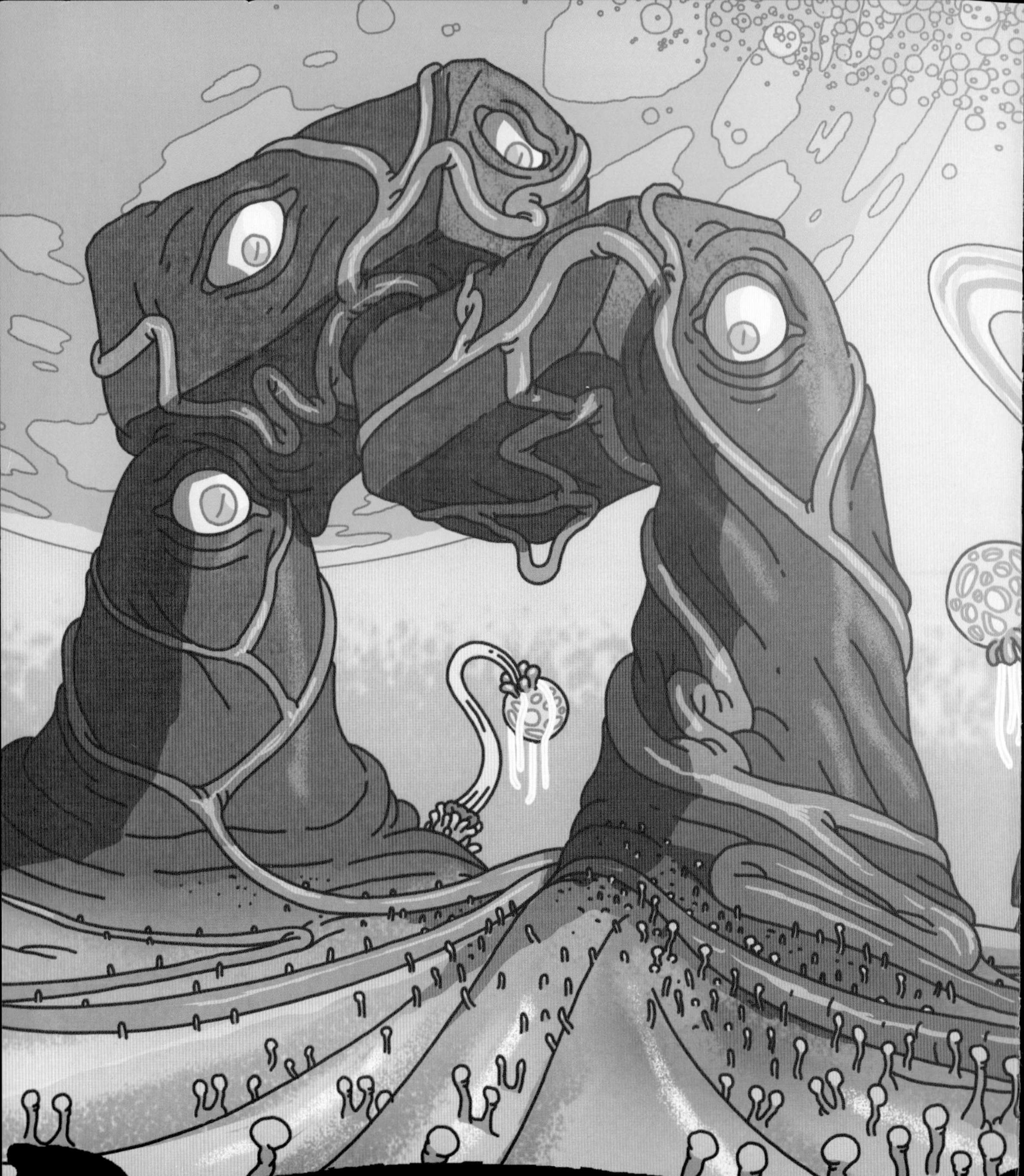

RICK AND MORTY CREATED BY
DAN HARMON AND JUSTIN ROILAND

WRITTEN BY
ZAC GORMAN

ILLUSTRATED BY
CJ CANNON

COLORED BY
RYAN HILL

BONUS SHORTS ART BY
MARC ELLERBY

LETTERED BY
CRANK!

ISSUE #5 INKED BY
CAT FARRIS

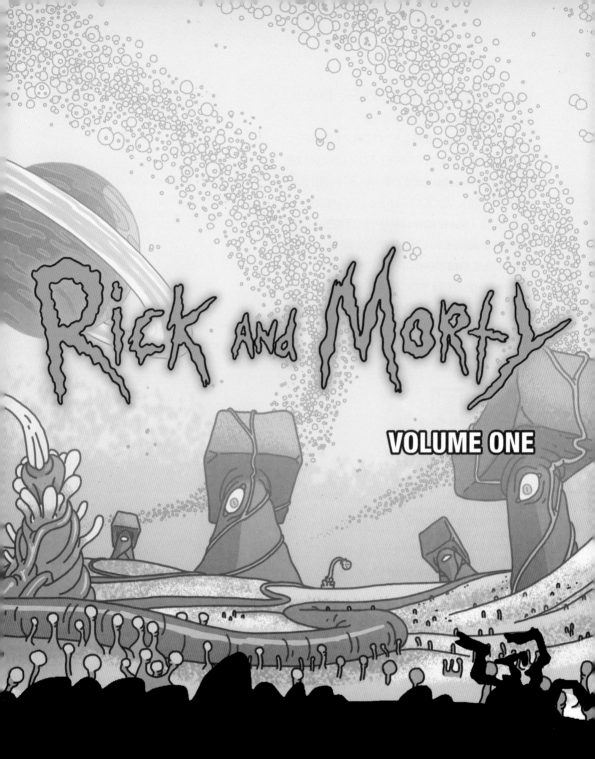

Rick and Morty

VOLUME ONE

EDITED BY
ARI YARWOOD

DESIGNED BY
HILARY THOMPSON

[adult swim]

PUBLISHED BY ONI PRESS, INC.

JOE NOZEMACK PUBLISHER

JAMES LUCAS JONES EDITOR IN CHIEF

CHEYENNE ALLOTT DIRECTOR OF SALES

FRED RECKLING DIRECTOR OF PUBLICITY

TROY LOOK PRODUCTION MANAGER

HILARY THOMPSON GRAPHIC DESIGNER

JARED JONES PRODUCTION ASSISTANT

CHARLIE CHU SENIOR EDITOR

ROBIN HERRERA EDITOR

ARI YARWOOD ASSOCIATE EDITOR

BRAD ROOKS INVENTORY COORDINATOR

JUNG LEE OFFICE ASSISTANT

[adult swim]™

ONIPRESS.COM
FACEBOOK.COM/ONIPRESS
TWITTER.COM/ONIPRESS
ONIPRESS.TUMBLR.COM
INSTAGRAM.COM/ONIPRESS
ADULTSWIM.COM
TWITTER.COM/RICKANDMORTY

THIS VOLUME COLLECTS ISSUES #1-5
OF THE ONI PRESS SERIES *RICK AND MORTY*.

FIRST EDITION: NOVEMBER 2015

RETAIL ISBN: 978-1-62010-281-7
BOOKS-A-MILLION EXCLUVSIVE ISBN: 978-1-62010-286-2
EISBN: 978-1-62010-282-4

PRINTED IN CHINA.

LIBRARY OF CONGRESS CONTROL NUMBER: 2015940219

1 2 3 4 5 6 7 8 9 10

SPECIAL THANKS TO JUSTIN ROILAND, DAN HARMON, MARISA MARIONAKIS, BRANDON LIVELY,
MIKE MENDEL, AND TAMARA HENDERSON.

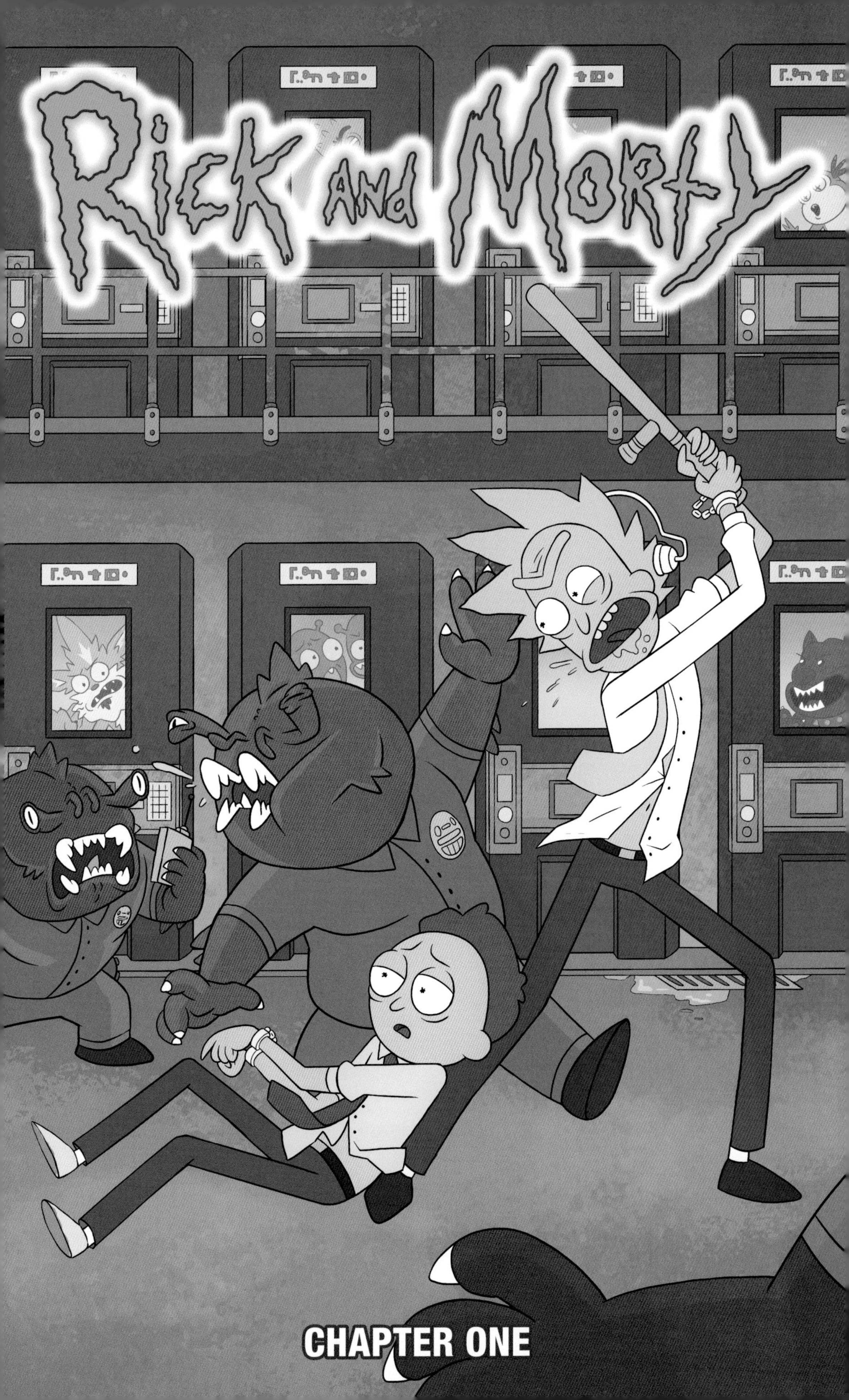
Rick and Morty
CHAPTER ONE

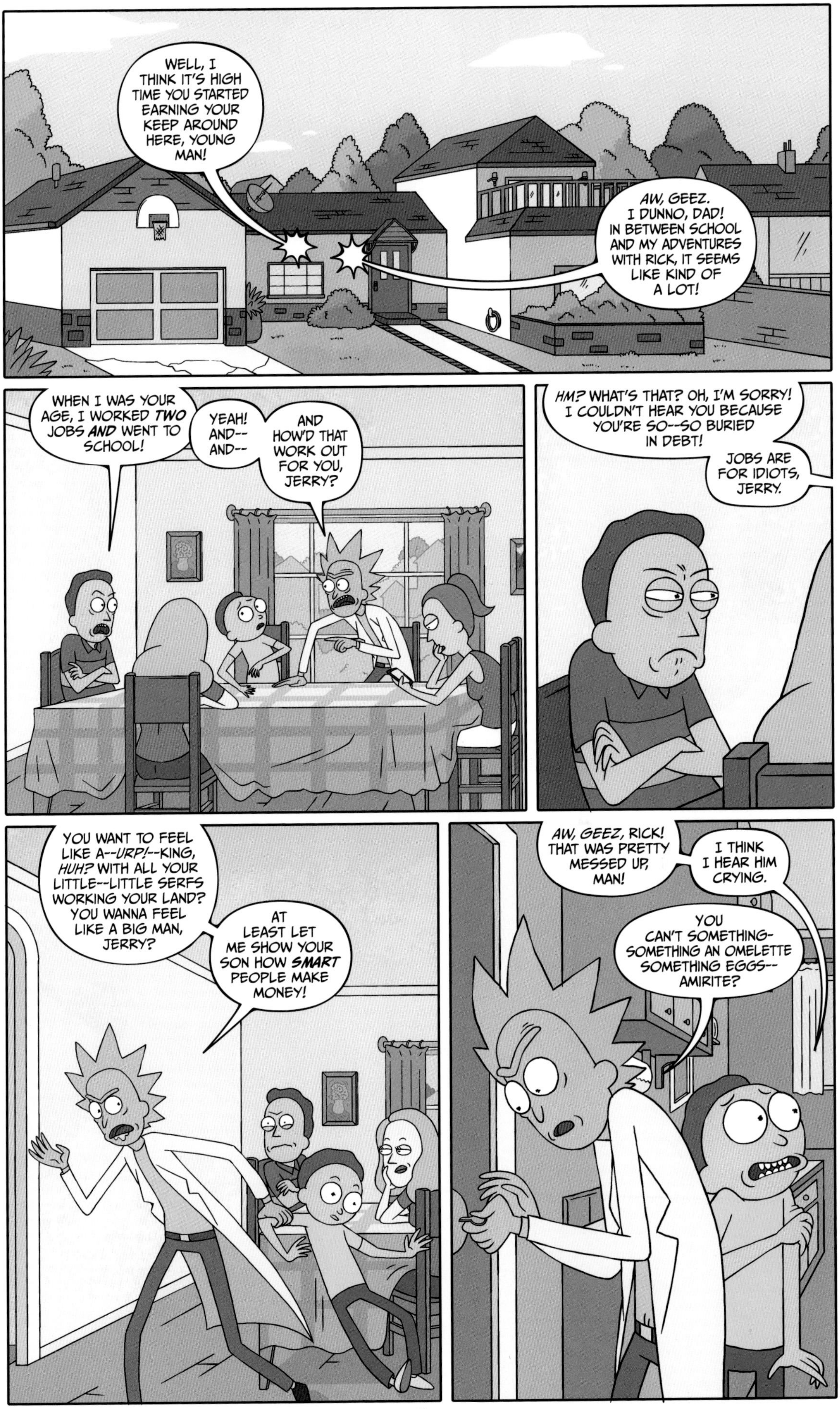

WELL, I THINK IT'S HIGH TIME YOU STARTED EARNING YOUR KEEP AROUND HERE, YOUNG MAN!
AW, GEEZ. I DUNNO, DAD! IN BETWEEN SCHOOL AND MY ADVENTURES WITH RICK, IT SEEMS LIKE KIND OF A LOT!
WHEN I WAS YOUR AGE, I WORKED *TWO* JOBS *AND* WENT TO SCHOOL!
YEAH! AND-- AND--
AND HOW'D THAT WORK OUT FOR YOU, JERRY?
HM? WHAT'S THAT? OH, I'M SORRY! I COULDN'T HEAR YOU BECAUSE YOU'RE SO--SO BURIED IN DEBT!
JOBS ARE FOR IDIOTS, JERRY.
YOU WANT TO FEEL LIKE A--*URP!*--KING, *HUH?* WITH ALL YOUR LITTLE--LITTLE SERFS WORKING YOUR LAND? YOU WANNA FEEL LIKE A BIG MAN, JERRY?
AT LEAST LET ME SHOW YOUR SON HOW *SMART* PEOPLE MAKE MONEY!
AW, GEEZ, RICK! THAT WAS PRETTY MESSED UP, MAN!
I THINK I HEAR HIM CRYING.
YOU CAN'T SOMETHING-SOMETHING AN OMELETTE SOMETHING EGGS--AMIRITE?

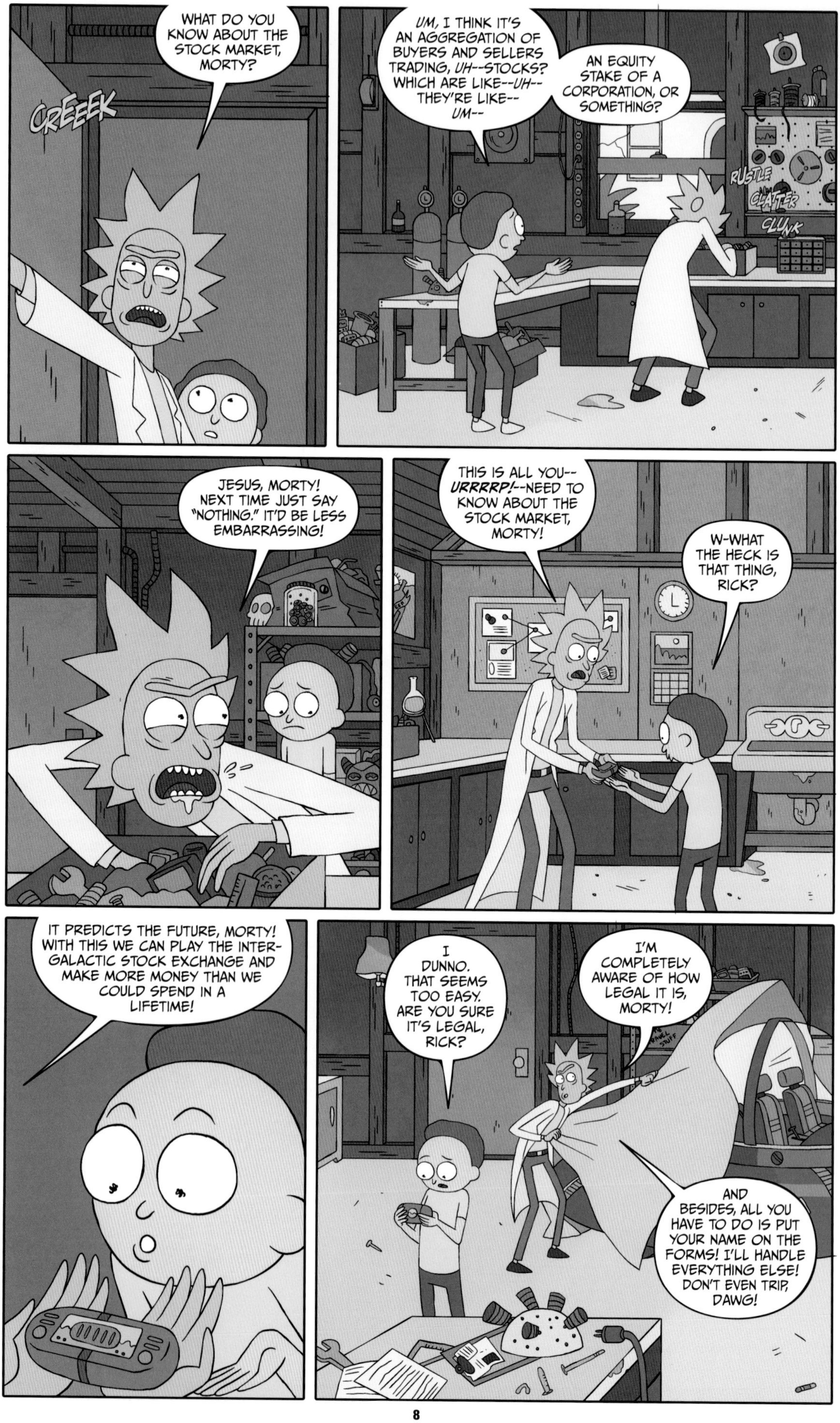
WHAT DO YOU KNOW ABOUT THE STOCK MARKET, MORTY?
CREEEK
UM, I THINK IT'S AN AGGREGATION OF BUYERS AND SELLERS TRADING, UH--STOCKS? WHICH ARE LIKE--UH-- THEY'RE LIKE-- UM--
AN EQUITY STAKE OF A CORPORATION, OR SOMETHING?
RUSTLE
CLATTER
CLUNK
JESUS, MORTY! NEXT TIME JUST SAY "NOTHING." IT'D BE LESS EMBARRASSING!
THIS IS ALL YOU-- URRRRP!--NEED TO KNOW ABOUT THE STOCK MARKET, MORTY!
W-WHAT THE HECK IS THAT THING, RICK?
IT PREDICTS THE FUTURE, MORTY! WITH THIS WE CAN PLAY THE INTER-GALACTIC STOCK EXCHANGE AND MAKE MORE MONEY THAN WE COULD SPEND IN A LIFETIME!
I DUNNO. THAT SEEMS TOO EASY. ARE YOU SURE IT'S LEGAL, RICK?
I'M COMPLETELY AWARE OF HOW LEGAL IT IS, MORTY!
AND BESIDES, ALL YOU HAVE TO DO IS PUT YOUR NAME ON THE FORMS! I'LL HANDLE EVERYTHING ELSE! DON'T EVEN TRIP, DAWG!

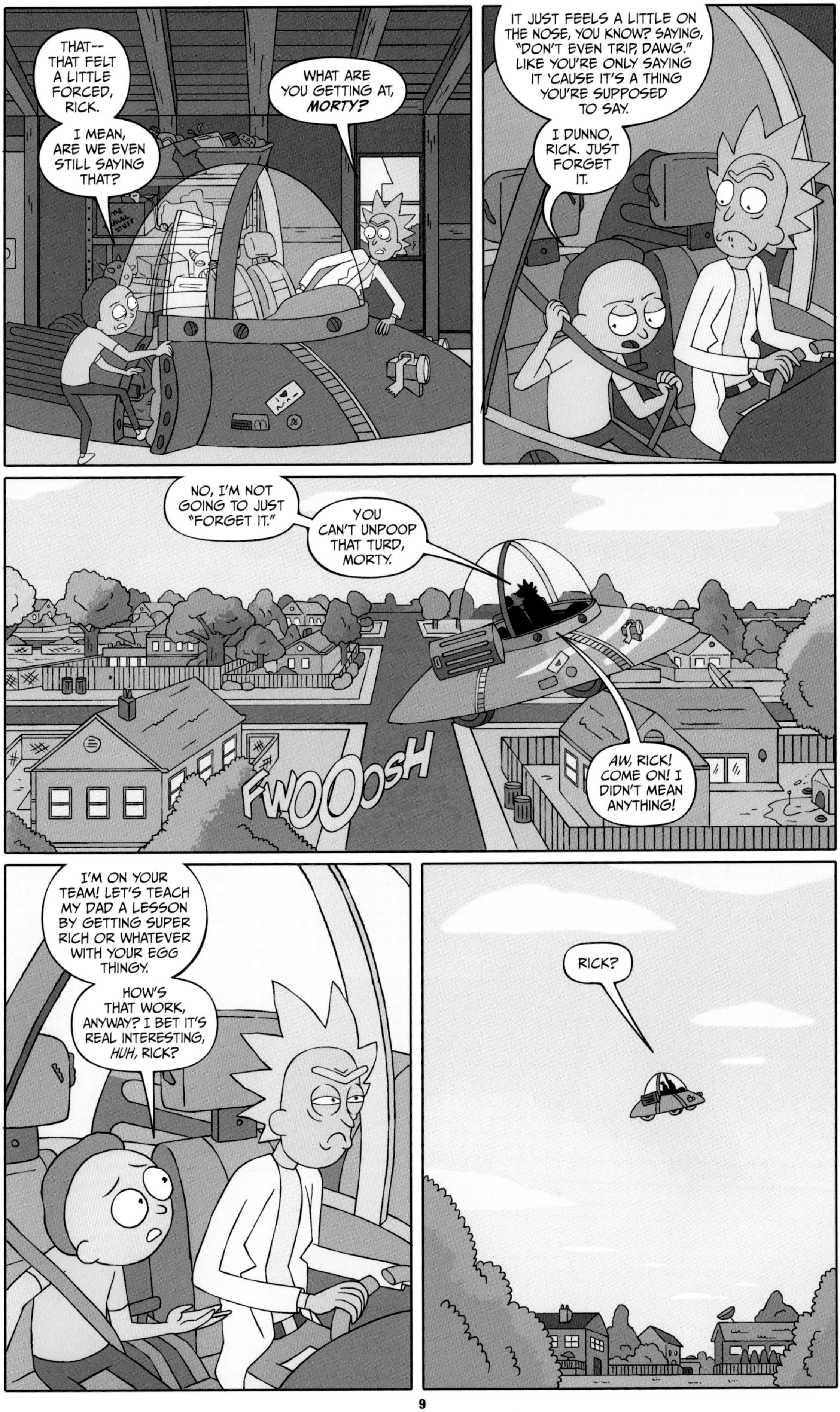
THAT-- THAT FELT A LITTLE FORCED, RICK.
I MEAN, ARE WE EVEN STILL SAYING THAT?
WHAT ARE YOU GETTING AT, *MORTY?*
IT JUST FEELS A LITTLE ON THE NOSE, YOU KNOW? SAYING, "DON'T EVEN TRIP, DAWG." LIKE YOU'RE ONLY SAYING IT 'CAUSE IT'S A THING YOU'RE SUPPOSED TO SAY.
I DUNNO, RICK. JUST FORGET IT.
NO, I'M NOT GOING TO JUST "FORGET IT."
YOU CAN'T UNPOOP THAT TURD, MORTY.
FWOOOSH
AW, RICK! COME ON! I DIDN'T MEAN ANYTHING!
I'M ON YOUR TEAM! LET'S TEACH MY DAD A LESSON BY GETTING SUPER RICH OR WHATEVER WITH YOUR EGG THINGY.
HOW'S THAT WORK, ANYWAY? I BET IT'S REAL INTERESTING, *HUH,* RICK?
RICK?

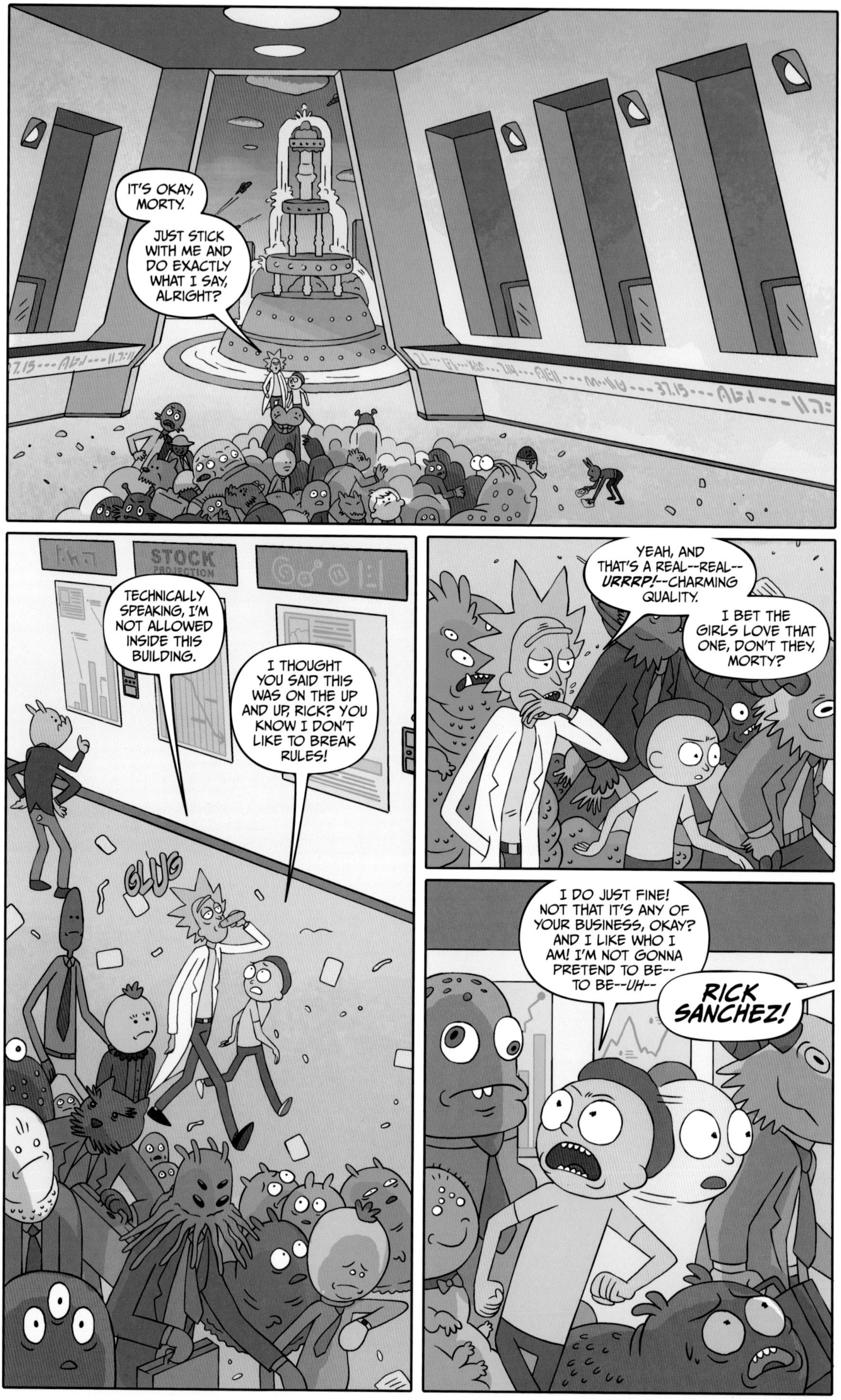
IT'S OKAY, MORTY.
JUST STICK WITH ME AND DO EXACTLY WHAT I SAY, ALRIGHT?
STOCK PROJECTION
TECHNICALLY SPEAKING, I'M NOT ALLOWED INSIDE THIS BUILDING.
I THOUGHT YOU SAID THIS WAS ON THE UP AND UP, RICK? YOU KNOW I DON'T LIKE TO BREAK RULES!
GLUG
YEAH, AND THAT'S A REAL--REAL--*URRRP!*--CHARMING QUALITY.
I BET THE GIRLS LOVE THAT ONE, DON'T THEY, MORTY?
I DO JUST FINE! NOT THAT IT'S ANY OF YOUR BUSINESS, OKAY? AND I LIKE WHO I AM! I'M NOT GONNA PRETEND TO BE-- TO BE--*UH*--
RICK SANCHEZ!

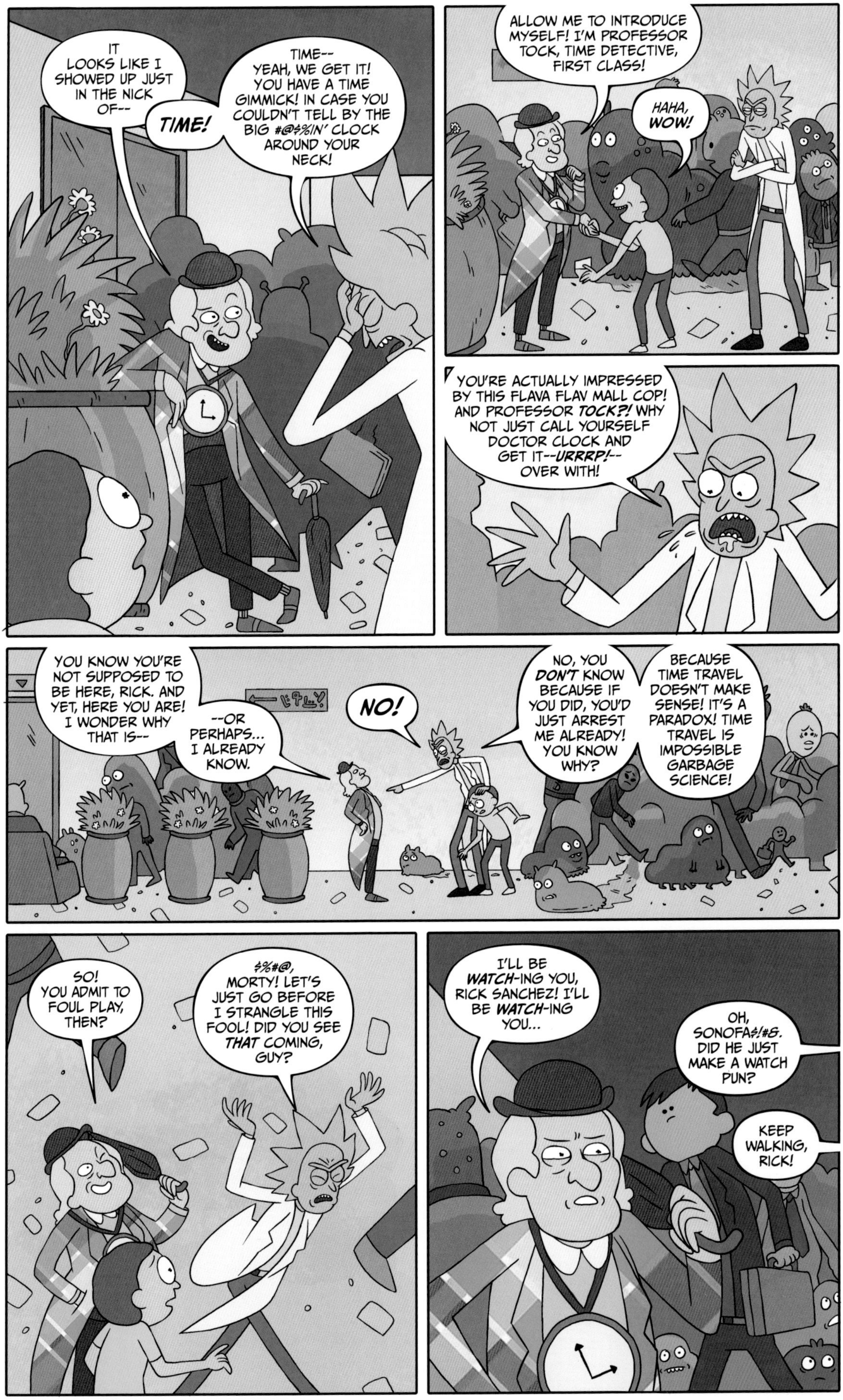
IT LOOKS LIKE I SHOWED UP JUST IN THE NICK OF--
TIME!
TIME-- YEAH, WE GET IT! YOU HAVE A TIME GIMMICK! IN CASE YOU COULDN'T TELL BY THE BIG #@$%IN' CLOCK AROUND YOUR NECK!
ALLOW ME TO INTRODUCE MYSELF! I'M PROFESSOR TOCK, TIME DETECTIVE, FIRST CLASS!
HAHA, WOW!
YOU'RE ACTUALLY IMPRESSED BY THIS FLAVA FLAV MALL COP! AND PROFESSOR TOCK?! WHY NOT JUST CALL YOURSELF DOCTOR CLOCK AND GET IT--URRRP!-- OVER WITH!
YOU KNOW YOU'RE NOT SUPPOSED TO BE HERE, RICK. AND YET, HERE YOU ARE! I WONDER WHY THAT IS--
--OR PERHAPS... I ALREADY KNOW.
NO!
NO, YOU DON'T KNOW BECAUSE IF YOU DID, YOU'D JUST ARREST ME ALREADY! YOU KNOW WHY?
BECAUSE TIME TRAVEL DOESN'T MAKE SENSE! IT'S A PARADOX! TIME TRAVEL IS IMPOSSIBLE GARBAGE SCIENCE!
SO! YOU ADMIT TO FOUL PLAY, THEN?
$%#@, MORTY! LET'S JUST GO BEFORE I STRANGLE THIS FOOL! DID YOU SEE THAT COMING, GUY?
I'LL BE WATCH-ING YOU, RICK SANCHEZ! I'LL BE WATCH-ING YOU...
OH, SONOFA$!#&. DID HE JUST MAKE A WATCH PUN?
KEEP WALKING, RICK!

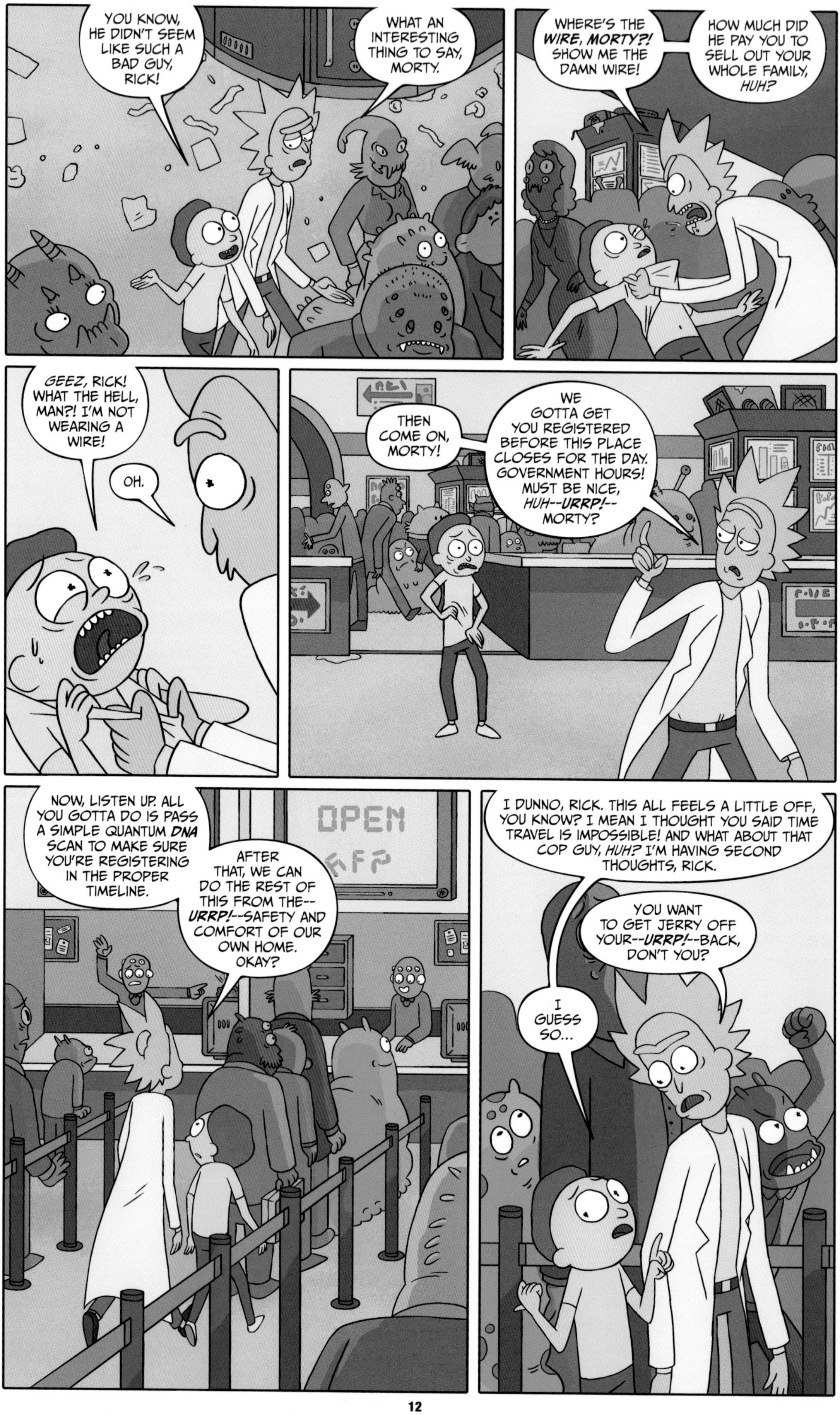
YOU KNOW, HE DIDN'T SEEM LIKE SUCH A BAD GUY, RICK!
WHAT AN INTERESTING THING TO SAY, MORTY.
WHERE'S THE *WIRE, MORTY?!* SHOW ME THE DAMN WIRE!
HOW MUCH DID HE PAY YOU TO SELL OUT YOUR WHOLE FAMILY, *HUH?*
GEEZ, RICK! WHAT THE HELL, MAN?! I'M NOT WEARING A WIRE!
OH.
THEN COME ON, MORTY!
WE GOTTA GET YOU REGISTERED BEFORE THIS PLACE CLOSES FOR THE DAY. GOVERNMENT HOURS! MUST BE NICE, *HUH--URRP!--* MORTY?
OPEN
NOW, LISTEN UP. ALL YOU GOTTA DO IS PASS A SIMPLE QUANTUM *DNA* SCAN TO MAKE SURE YOU'RE REGISTERING IN THE PROPER TIMELINE.
AFTER THAT, WE CAN DO THE REST OF THIS FROM THE-- *URRP!*--SAFETY AND COMFORT OF OUR OWN HOME. OKAY?
I DUNNO, RICK. THIS ALL FEELS A LITTLE OFF, YOU KNOW? I MEAN I THOUGHT YOU SAID TIME TRAVEL IS IMPOSSIBLE! AND WHAT ABOUT THAT COP GUY, *HUH?* I'M HAVING SECOND THOUGHTS, RICK.
YOU WANT TO GET JERRY OFF YOUR--*URRP!*--BACK, DON'T YOU?
I GUESS SO...

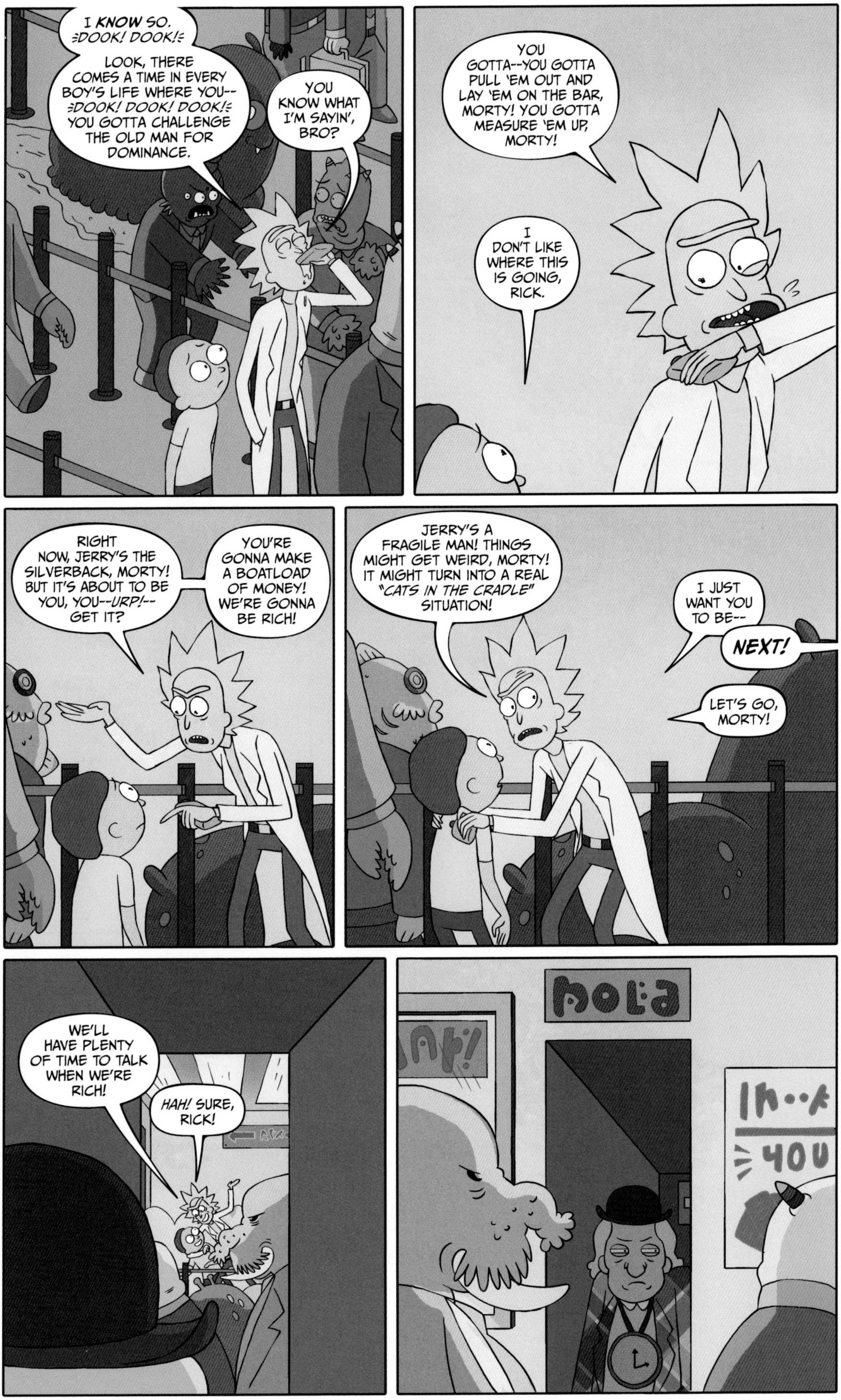
I KNOW SO. ⩶DOOK! DOOK!⩶
LOOK, THERE COMES A TIME IN EVERY BOY'S LIFE WHERE YOU-- ⩶DOOK! DOOK! DOOK!⩶ YOU GOTTA CHALLENGE THE OLD MAN FOR DOMINANCE.
YOU KNOW WHAT I'M SAYIN', BRO?
YOU GOTTA--YOU GOTTA PULL 'EM OUT AND LAY 'EM ON THE BAR, MORTY! YOU GOTTA MEASURE 'EM UP, MORTY!
I DON'T LIKE WHERE THIS IS GOING, RICK.
RIGHT NOW, JERRY'S THE SILVERBACK, MORTY! BUT IT'S ABOUT TO BE YOU, YOU--URP!-- GET IT?
YOU'RE GONNA MAKE A BOATLOAD OF MONEY! WE'RE GONNA BE RICH!
JERRY'S A FRAGILE MAN! THINGS MIGHT GET WEIRD, MORTY! IT MIGHT TURN INTO A REAL "CATS IN THE CRADLE" SITUATION!
I JUST WANT YOU TO BE--
NEXT!
LET'S GO, MORTY!
WE'LL HAVE PLENTY OF TIME TO TALK WHEN WE'RE RICH!
HAH! SURE, RICK!

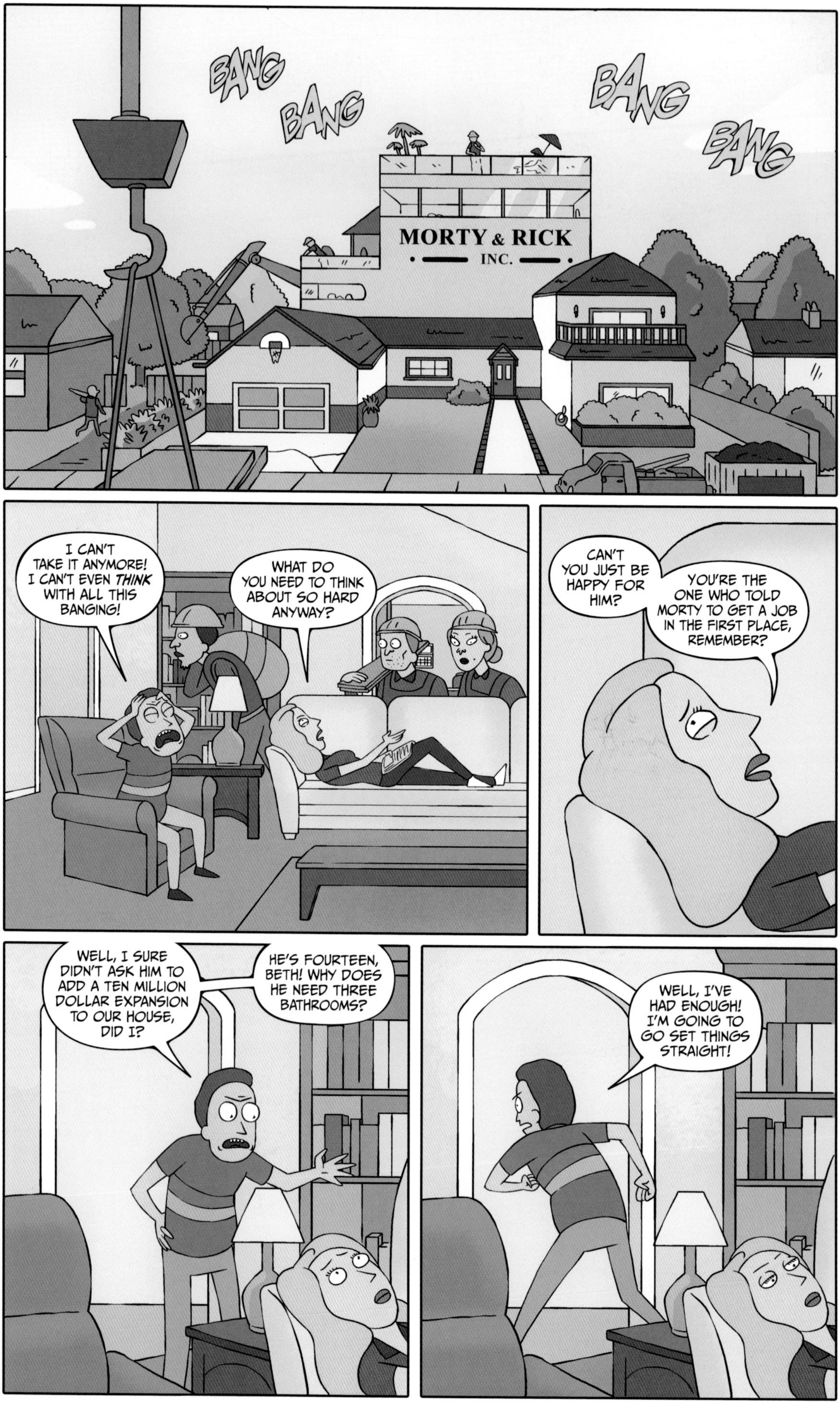
BANG
BANG
MORTY & RICK INC.
BANG
BANG
I CAN'T TAKE IT ANYMORE! I CAN'T EVEN *THINK* WITH ALL THIS BANGING!
WHAT DO YOU NEED TO THINK ABOUT SO HARD ANYWAY?
CAN'T YOU JUST BE HAPPY FOR HIM?
YOU'RE THE ONE WHO TOLD MORTY TO GET A JOB IN THE FIRST PLACE, REMEMBER?
WELL, I SURE DIDN'T ASK HIM TO ADD A TEN MILLION DOLLAR EXPANSION TO OUR HOUSE, DID I?
HE'S FOURTEEN, BETH! WHY DOES HE NEED THREE BATHROOMS?
WELL, I'VE HAD ENOUGH! I'M GOING TO GO SET THINGS STRAIGHT!

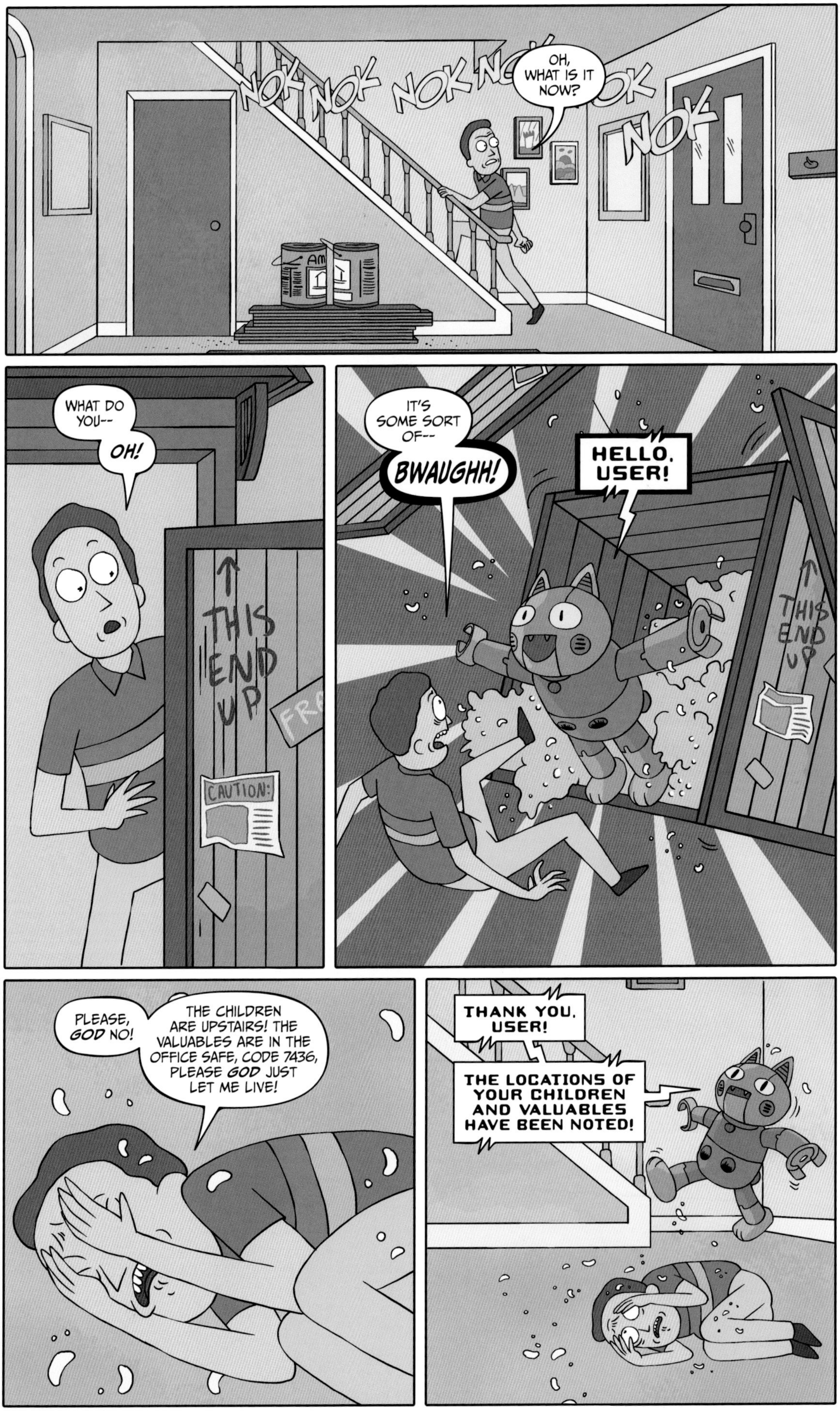

NOK NOK NOK NOK NOK NOK
OH, WHAT IS IT NOW?
WHAT DO YOU-- OH!
THIS END UP
CAUTION:
IT'S SOME SORT OF-- BWAUGHH!
HELLO, USER!
THIS END UP
PLEASE, GOD NO!
THE CHILDREN ARE UPSTAIRS! THE VALUABLES ARE IN THE OFFICE SAFE, CODE 7436, PLEASE GOD JUST LET ME LIVE!
THANK YOU, USER!
THE LOCATIONS OF YOUR CHILDREN AND VALUABLES HAVE BEEN NOTED!

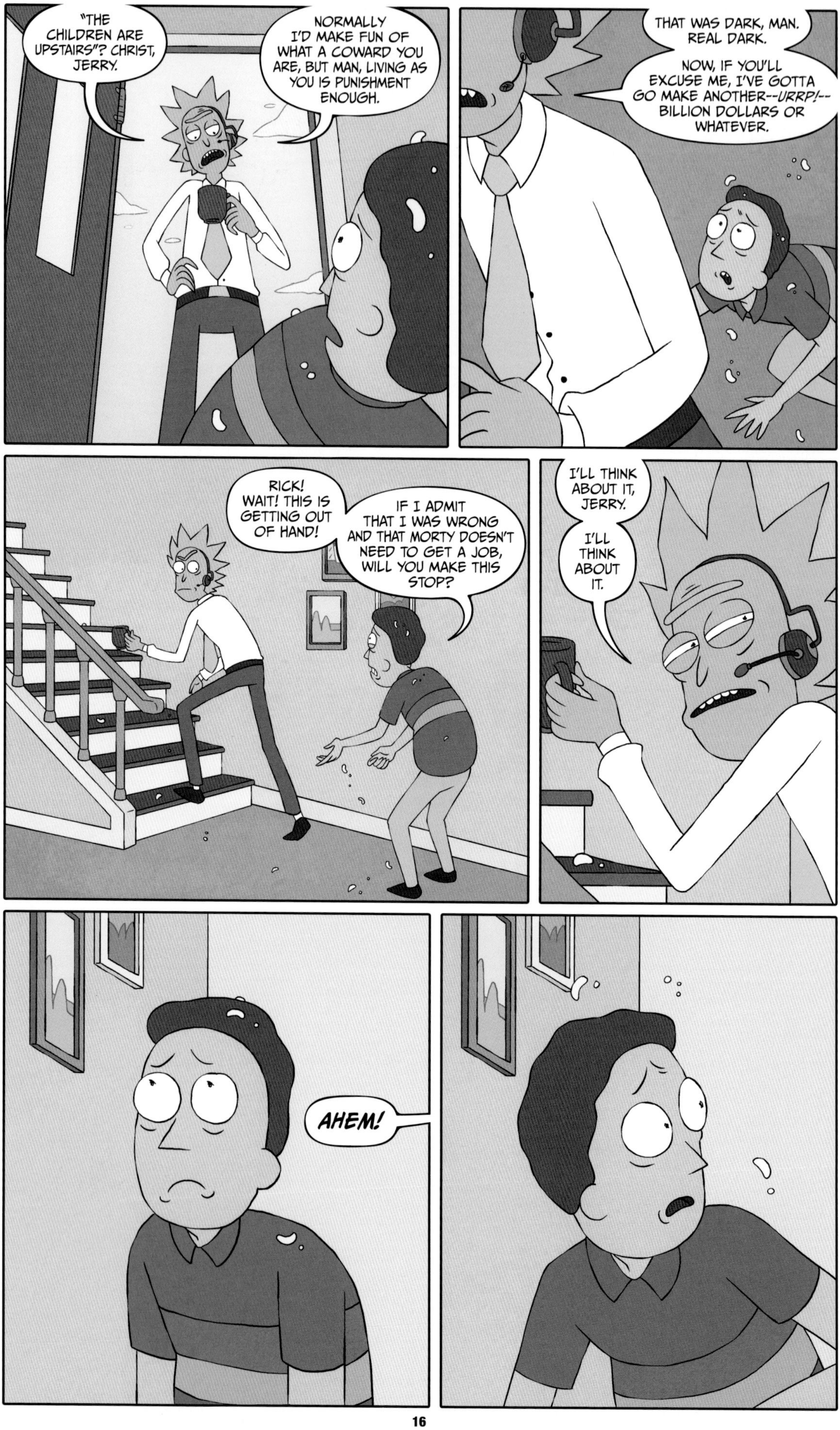
"THE CHILDREN ARE UPSTAIRS"? CHRIST, JERRY.
NORMALLY I'D MAKE FUN OF WHAT A COWARD YOU ARE, BUT MAN, LIVING AS YOU IS PUNISHMENT ENOUGH.
THAT WAS DARK, MAN. REAL DARK.
NOW, IF YOU'LL EXCUSE ME, I'VE GOTTA GO MAKE ANOTHER--URRP!--BILLION DOLLARS OR WHATEVER.
RICK! WAIT! THIS IS GETTING OUT OF HAND!
IF I ADMIT THAT I WAS WRONG AND THAT MORTY DOESN'T NEED TO GET A JOB, WILL YOU MAKE THIS STOP?
I'LL THINK ABOUT IT, JERRY.
I'LL THINK ABOUT IT.
AHEM!

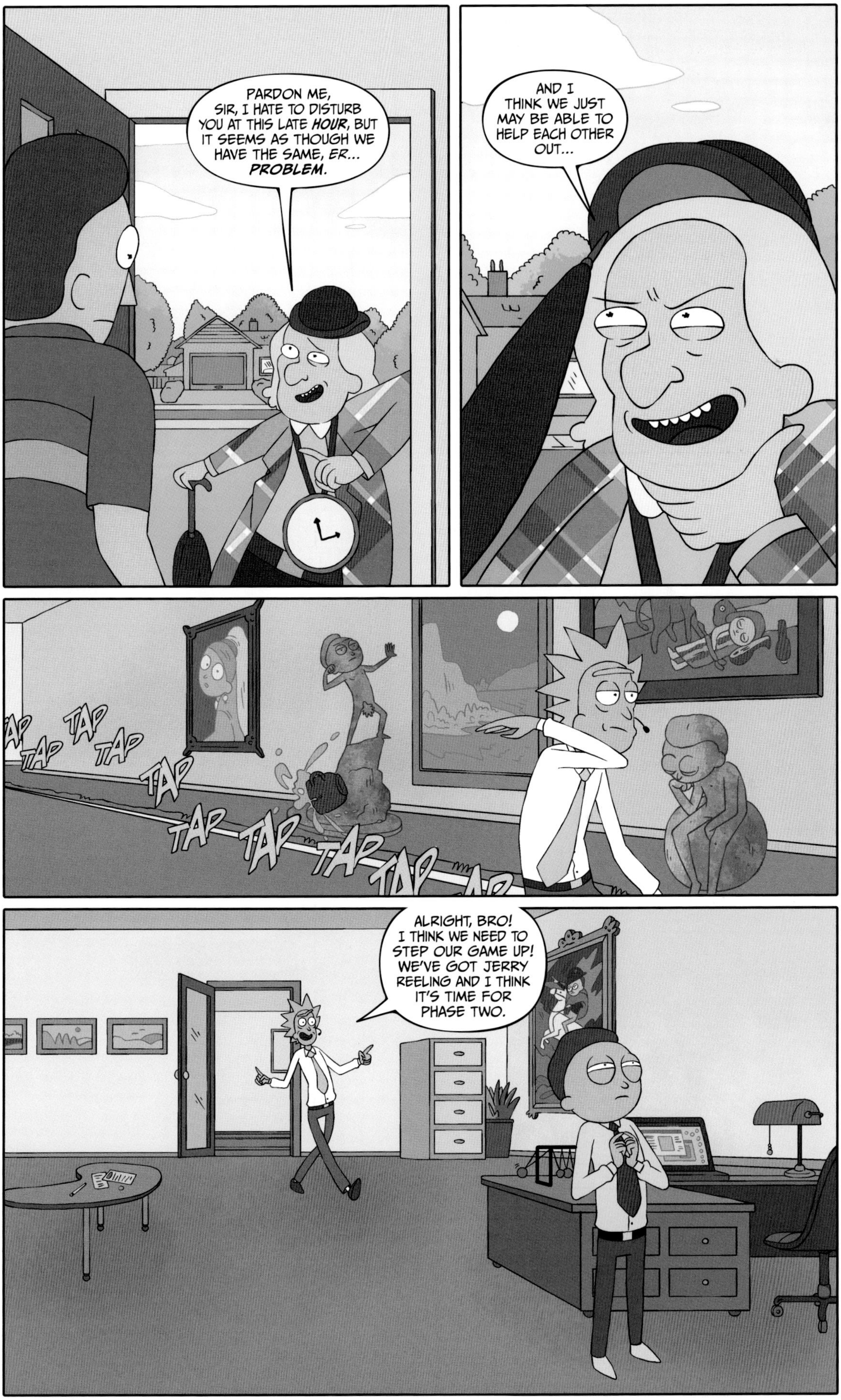
PARDON ME, SIR, I HATE TO DISTURB YOU AT THIS LATE *HOUR*, BUT IT SEEMS AS THOUGH WE HAVE THE SAME, *ER*... ***PROBLEM***.
AND I THINK WE JUST MAY BE ABLE TO HELP EACH OTHER OUT...
TAP TAP TAP TAP TAP TAP TAP TAP TAP
ALRIGHT, BRO! I THINK WE NEED TO STEP OUR GAME UP! WE'VE GOT JERRY REELING AND I THINK IT'S TIME FOR PHASE TWO.

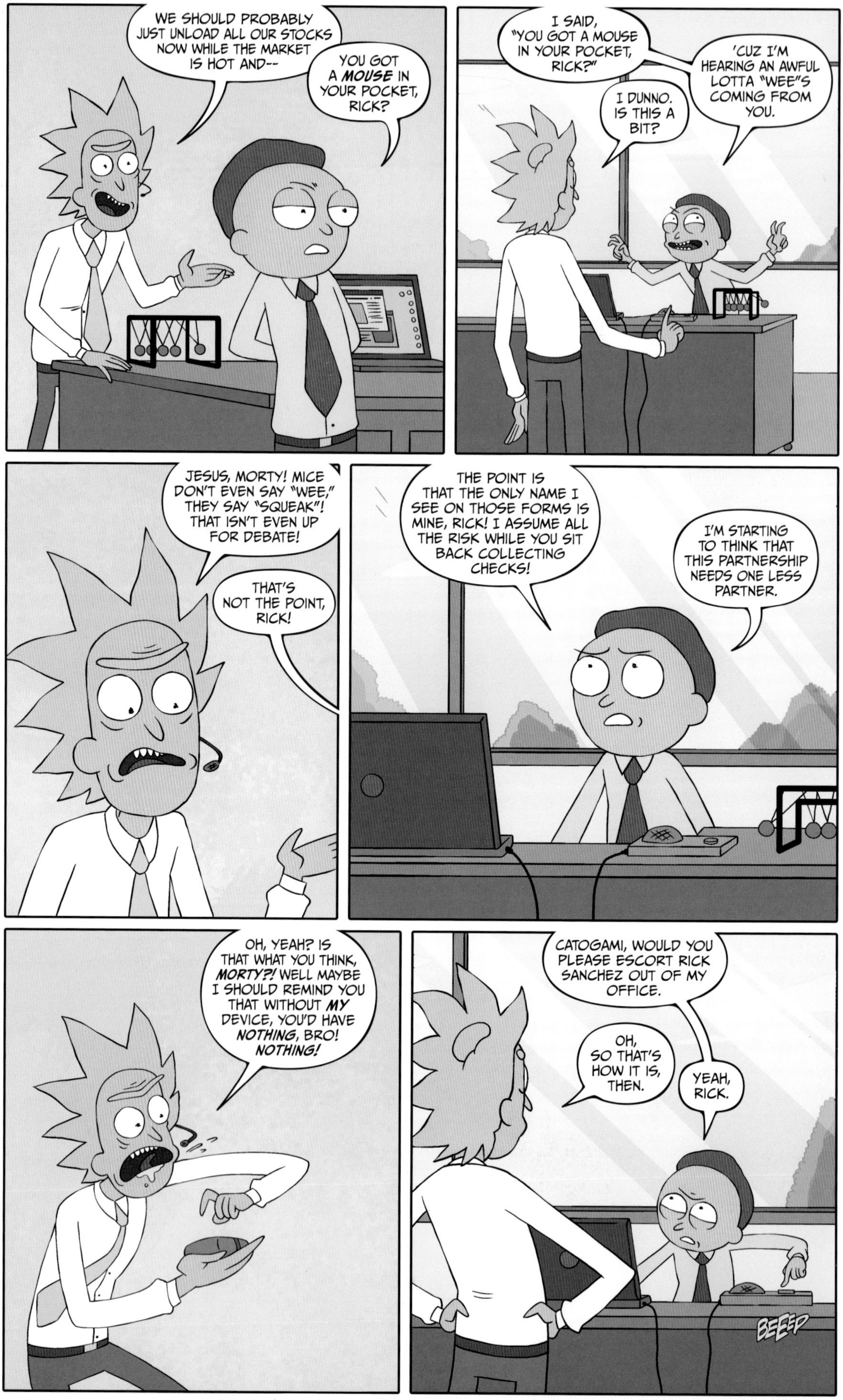
WE SHOULD PROBABLY JUST UNLOAD ALL OUR STOCKS NOW WHILE THE MARKET IS HOT AND--
YOU GOT A **MOUSE** IN YOUR POCKET, RICK?
I SAID, "YOU GOT A MOUSE IN YOUR POCKET, RICK?"
'CUZ I'M HEARING AN AWFUL LOTTA "WEE"S COMING FROM YOU.
I DUNNO. IS THIS A BIT?
JESUS, MORTY! MICE DON'T EVEN SAY "WEE," THEY SAY "SQUEAK"! THAT ISN'T EVEN UP FOR DEBATE!
THAT'S NOT THE POINT, RICK!
THE POINT IS THAT THE ONLY NAME I SEE ON THOSE FORMS IS MINE, RICK! I ASSUME ALL THE RISK WHILE YOU SIT BACK COLLECTING CHECKS!
I'M STARTING TO THINK THAT THIS PARTNERSHIP NEEDS ONE LESS PARTNER.
OH, YEAH? IS THAT WHAT YOU THINK, ***MORTY?!*** WELL MAYBE I SHOULD REMIND YOU THAT WITHOUT ***MY*** DEVICE, YOU'D HAVE ***NOTHING***, BRO! ***NOTHING!***
CATOGAMI, WOULD YOU PLEASE ESCORT RICK SANCHEZ OUT OF MY OFFICE.
OH, SO THAT'S HOW IT IS, THEN.
YEAH, RICK.
BEEEP

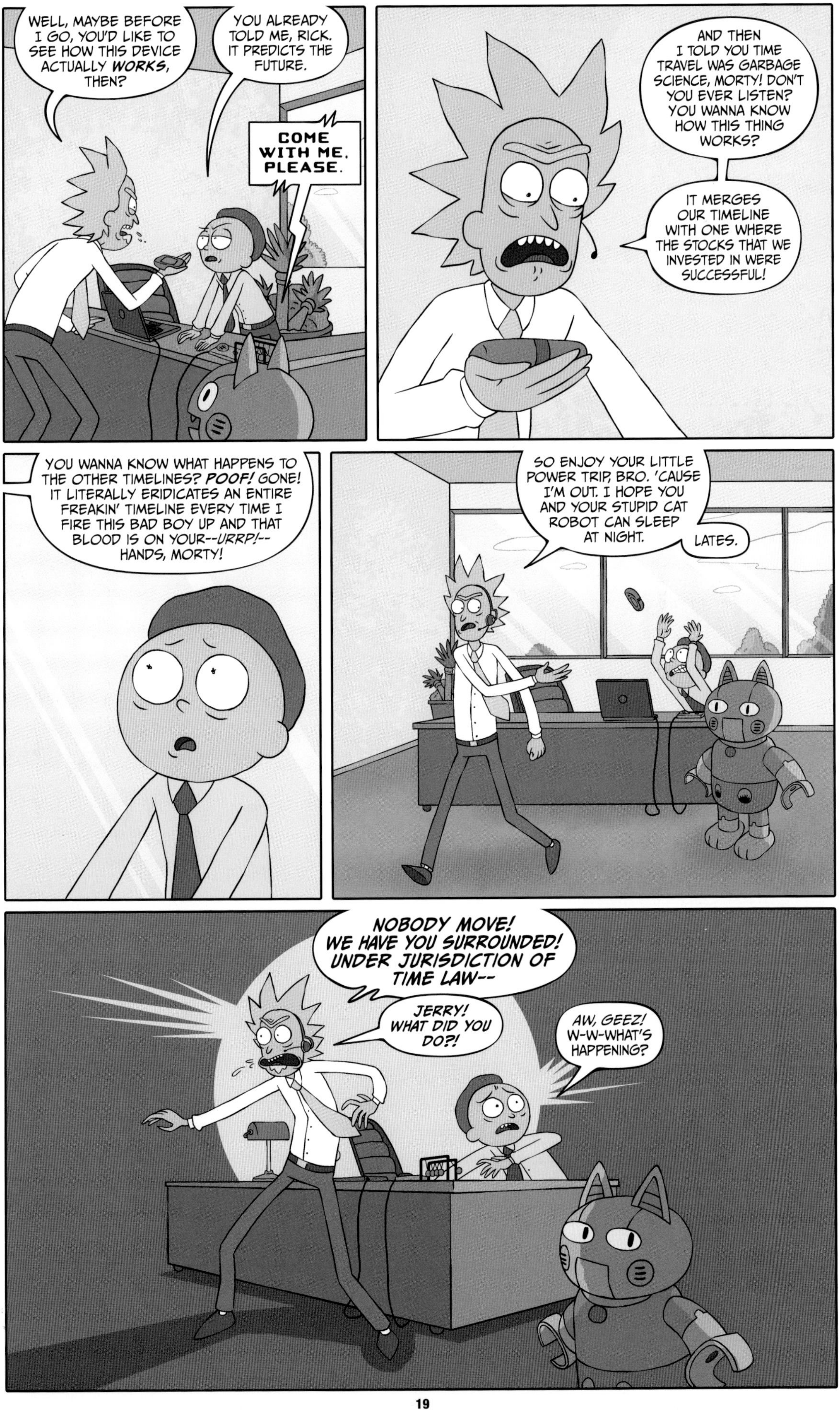
WELL, MAYBE BEFORE I GO, YOU'D LIKE TO SEE HOW THIS DEVICE ACTUALLY **WORKS**, THEN?
YOU ALREADY TOLD ME, RICK. IT PREDICTS THE FUTURE.
COME WITH ME, PLEASE.
AND THEN I TOLD YOU TIME TRAVEL WAS GARBAGE SCIENCE, MORTY! DON'T YOU EVER LISTEN? YOU WANNA KNOW HOW THIS THING WORKS?
IT MERGES OUR TIMELINE WITH ONE WHERE THE STOCKS THAT WE INVESTED IN WERE SUCCESSFUL!
YOU WANNA KNOW WHAT HAPPENS TO THE OTHER TIMELINES? ***POOF!*** GONE! IT LITERALLY ERIDICATES AN ENTIRE FREAKIN' TIMELINE EVERY TIME I FIRE THIS BAD BOY UP AND THAT BLOOD IS ON YOUR--*URRP!*--HANDS, MORTY!
SO ENJOY YOUR LITTLE POWER TRIP, BRO. 'CAUSE I'M OUT. I HOPE YOU AND YOUR STUPID CAT ROBOT CAN SLEEP AT NIGHT.
LATES.
NOBODY MOVE! WE HAVE YOU SURROUNDED! UNDER JURISDICTION OF TIME LAW--
JERRY! WHAT DID YOU DO?!
AW, GEEZ! W-W-WHAT'S HAPPENING?

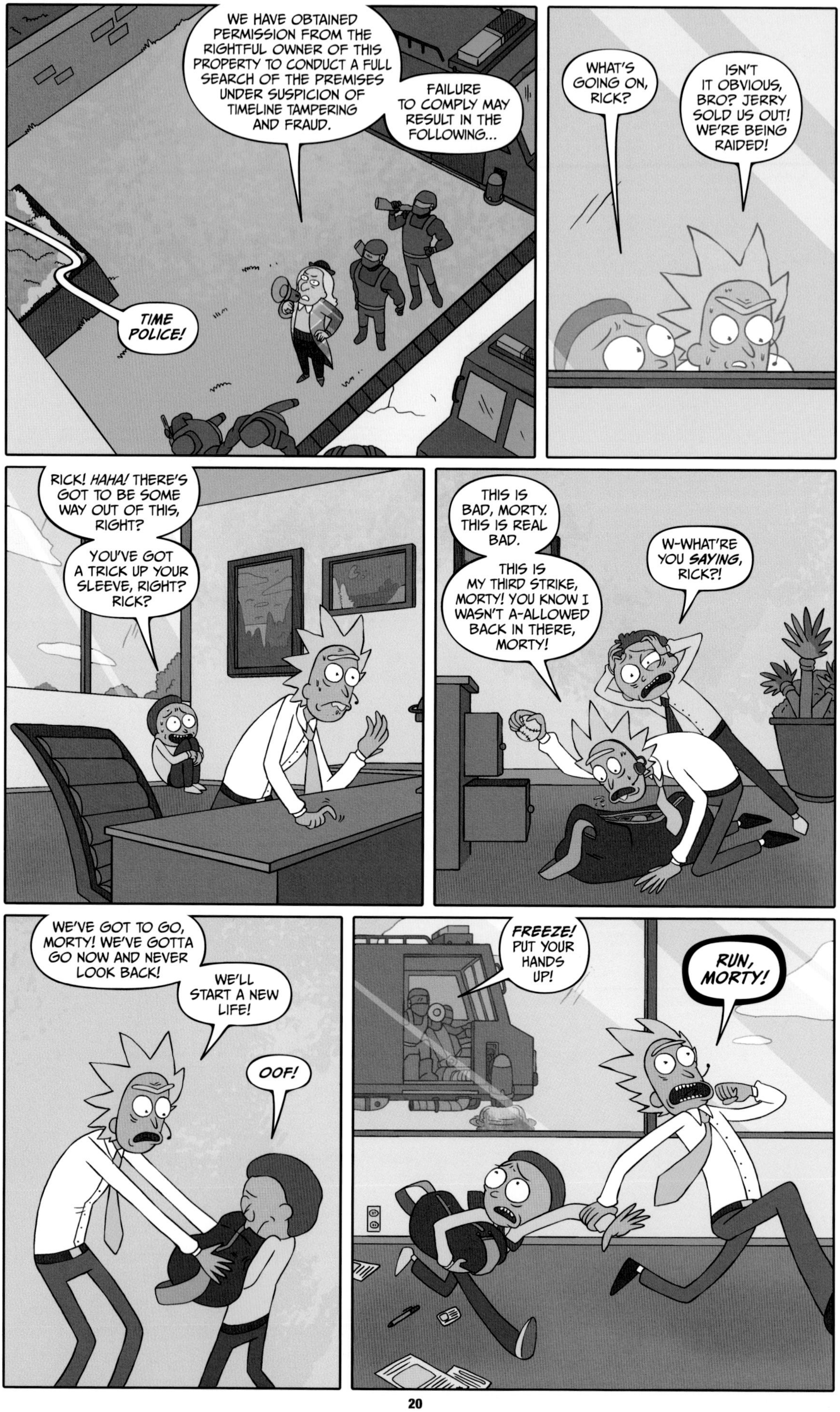

WE HAVE OBTAINED PERMISSION FROM THE RIGHTFUL OWNER OF THIS PROPERTY TO CONDUCT A FULL SEARCH OF THE PREMISES UNDER SUSPICION OF TIMELINE TAMPERING AND FRAUD.
FAILURE TO COMPLY MAY RESULT IN THE FOLLOWING...
TIME POLICE!
WHAT'S GOING ON, RICK?
ISN'T IT OBVIOUS, BRO? JERRY SOLD US OUT! WE'RE BEING RAIDED!
RICK! *HAHA!* THERE'S GOT TO BE SOME WAY OUT OF THIS, RIGHT?
YOU'VE GOT A TRICK UP YOUR SLEEVE, RIGHT? RICK?
THIS IS BAD, MORTY. THIS IS REAL BAD.
THIS IS MY THIRD STRIKE, MORTY! YOU KNOW I WASN'T A-ALLOWED BACK IN THERE, MORTY!
W-WHAT'RE YOU *SAYING*, RICK?!
WE'VE GOT TO GO, MORTY! WE'VE GOTTA GO NOW AND NEVER LOOK BACK!
WE'LL START A NEW LIFE!
OOF!
FREEZE! PUT YOUR HANDS UP!
RUN, MORTY!

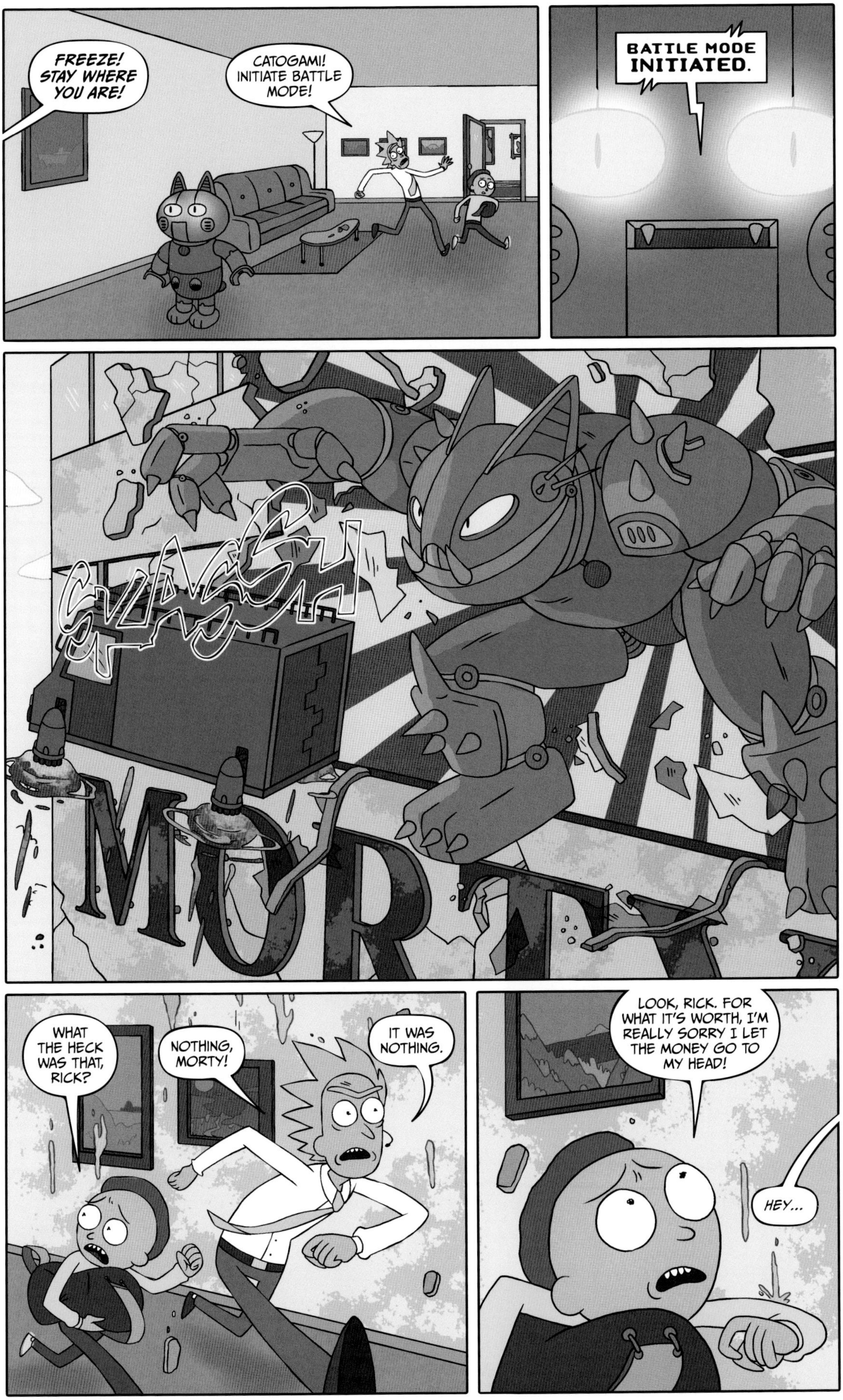
FREEZE! STAY WHERE YOU ARE!
CATOGAMI! INITIATE BATTLE MODE!
BATTLE MODE INITIATED.
SMASH
WHAT THE HECK WAS THAT, RICK?
NOTHING, MORTY!
IT WAS NOTHING.
LOOK, RICK. FOR WHAT IT'S WORTH, I'M REALLY SORRY I LET THE MONEY GO TO MY HEAD!
HEY...

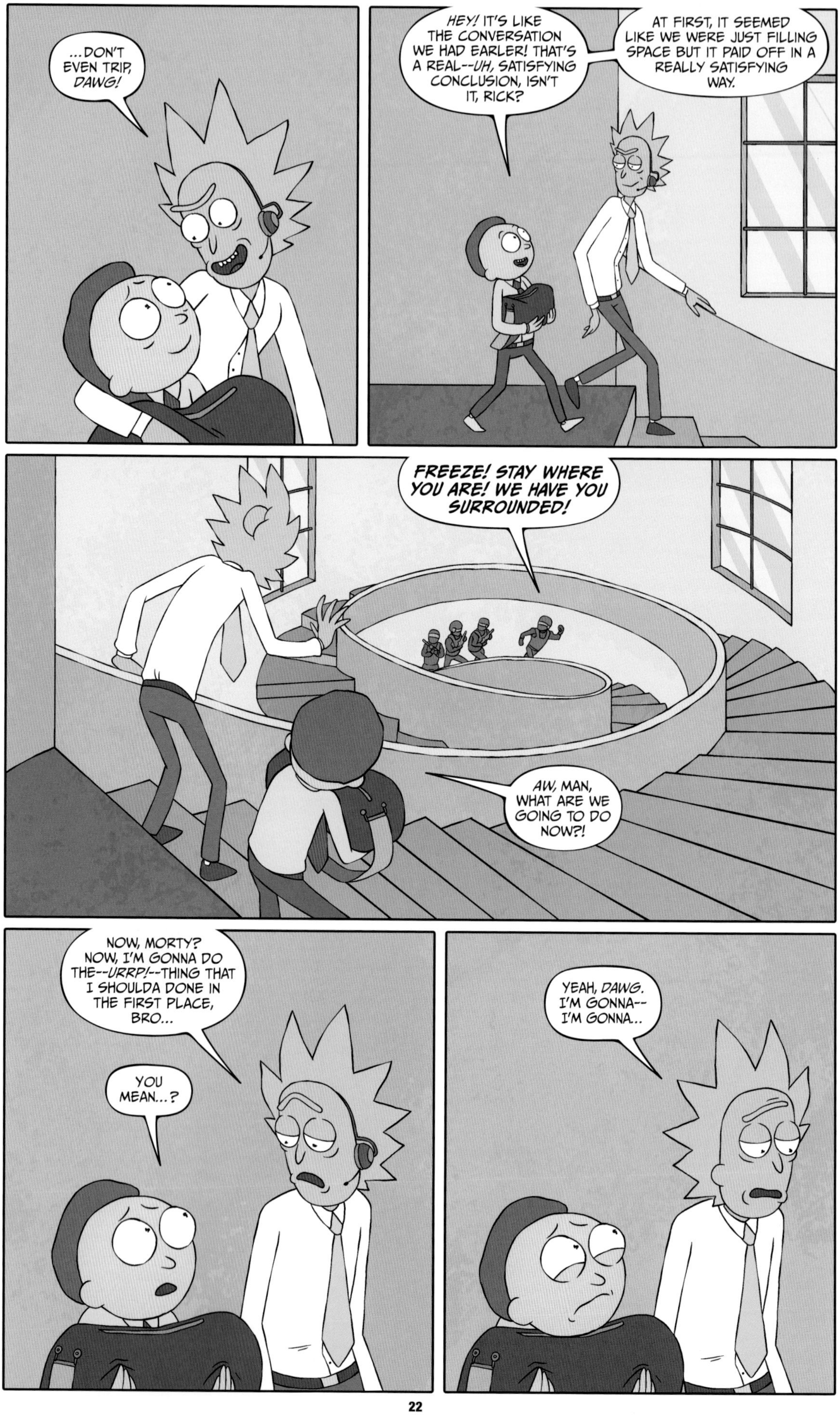
...DON'T EVEN TRIP, DAWG!
HEY! IT'S LIKE THE CONVERSATION WE HAD EARLER! THAT'S A REAL--UH, SATISFYING CONCLUSION, ISN'T IT, RICK?
AT FIRST, IT SEEMED LIKE WE WERE JUST FILLING SPACE BUT IT PAID OFF IN A REALLY SATISFYING WAY.
FREEZE! STAY WHERE YOU ARE! WE HAVE YOU SURROUNDED!
AW, MAN, WHAT ARE WE GOING TO DO NOW?!
NOW, MORTY? NOW, I'M GONNA DO THE--URRP!--THING THAT I SHOULDA DONE IN THE FIRST PLACE, BRO...
YOU MEAN...?
YEAH, DAWG. I'M GONNA-- I'M GONNA...

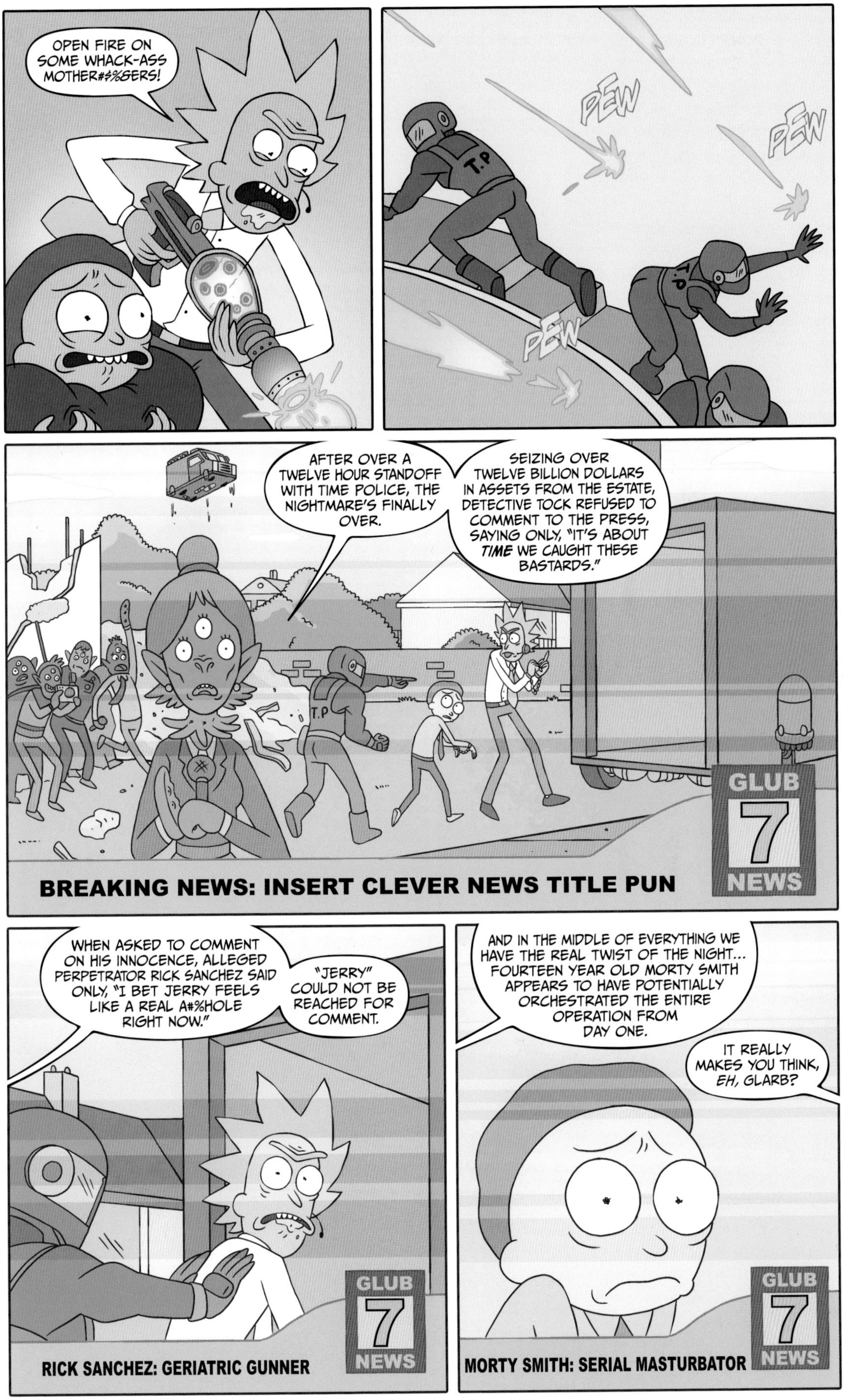

OPEN FIRE ON SOME WHACK-ASS MOTHER#$%&GERS!
PEW
PEW
PEW
AFTER OVER A TWELVE HOUR STANDOFF WITH TIME POLICE, THE NIGHTMARE'S FINALLY OVER.
SEIZING OVER TWELVE BILLION DOLLARS IN ASSETS FROM THE ESTATE, DETECTIVE TOCK REFUSED TO COMMENT TO THE PRESS, SAYING ONLY, "IT'S ABOUT *TIME* WE CAUGHT THESE BASTARDS."
T.P
GLUB 7 NEWS
BREAKING NEWS: INSERT CLEVER NEWS TITLE PUN
WHEN ASKED TO COMMENT ON HIS INNOCENCE, ALLEGED PERPETRATOR RICK SANCHEZ SAID ONLY, "I BET JERRY FEELS LIKE A REAL A#%HOLE RIGHT NOW."
"JERRY" COULD NOT BE REACHED FOR COMMENT.
GLUB 7 NEWS
RICK SANCHEZ: GERIATRIC GUNNER
AND IN THE MIDDLE OF EVERYTHING WE HAVE THE REAL TWIST OF THE NIGHT... FOURTEEN YEAR OLD MORTY SMITH APPEARS TO HAVE POTENTIALLY ORCHESTRATED THE ENTIRE OPERATION FROM DAY ONE.
IT REALLY MAKES YOU THINK, *EH,* GLARB?
GLUB 7 NEWS
MORTY SMITH: SERIAL MASTURBATOR

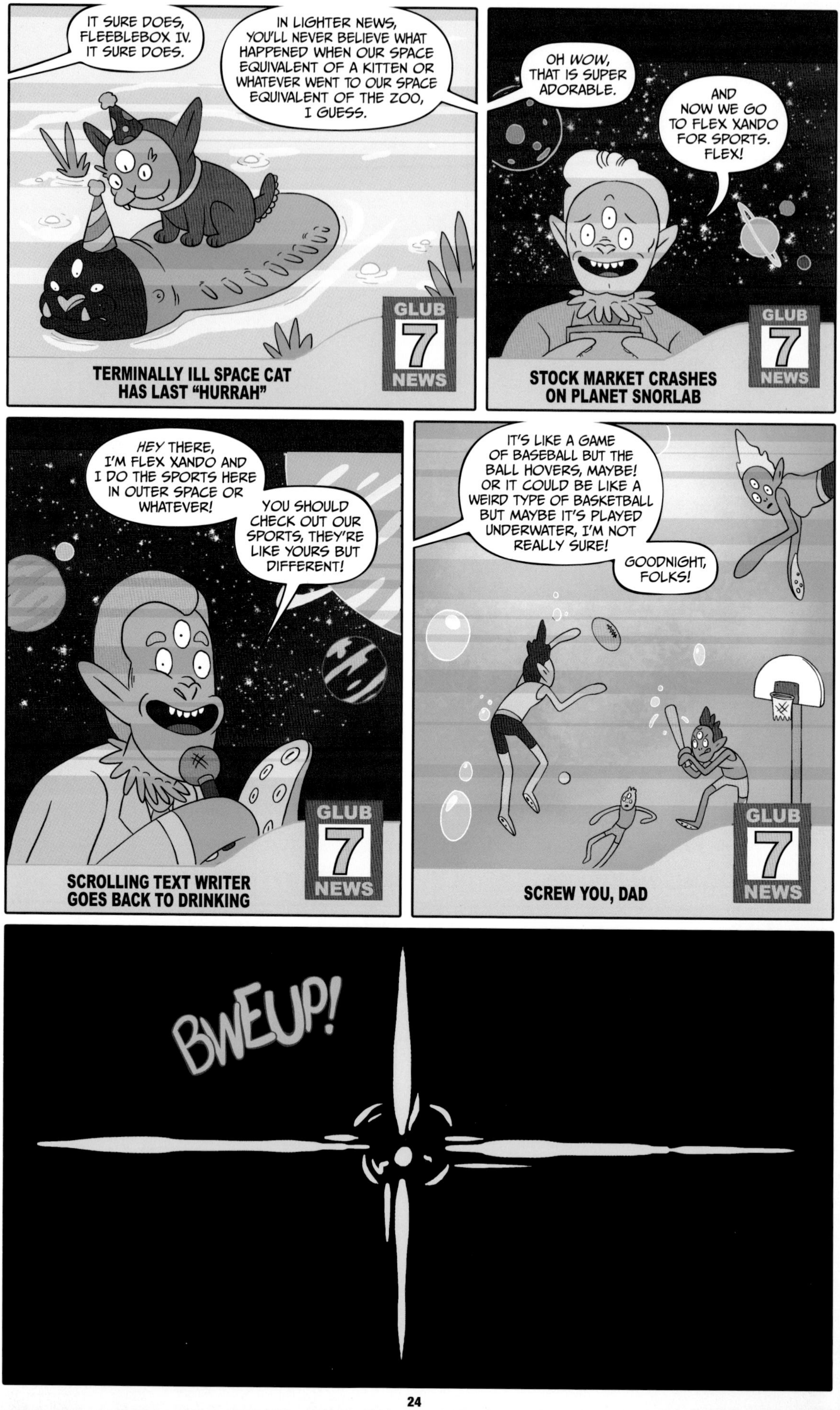
IT SURE DOES, FLEEBLEBOX IV. IT SURE DOES.
IN LIGHTER NEWS, YOU'LL NEVER BELIEVE WHAT HAPPENED WHEN OUR SPACE EQUIVALENT OF A KITTEN OR WHATEVER WENT TO OUR SPACE EQUIVALENT OF THE ZOO, I GUESS.
GLUB 7 NEWS
TERMINALLY ILL SPACE CAT HAS LAST "HURRAH"
OH WOW, THAT IS SUPER ADORABLE.
AND NOW WE GO TO FLEX XANDO FOR SPORTS. FLEX!
GLUB 7 NEWS
STOCK MARKET CRASHES ON PLANET SNORLAB
HEY THERE, I'M FLEX XANDO AND I DO THE SPORTS HERE IN OUTER SPACE OR WHATEVER!
YOU SHOULD CHECK OUT OUR SPORTS, THEY'RE LIKE YOURS BUT DIFFERENT!
GLUB 7 NEWS
SCROLLING TEXT WRITER GOES BACK TO DRINKING
IT'S LIKE A GAME OF BASEBALL BUT THE BALL HOVERS, MAYBE! OR IT COULD BE LIKE A WEIRD TYPE OF BASKETBALL BUT MAYBE IT'S PLAYED UNDERWATER, I'M NOT REALLY SURE!
GOODNIGHT, FOLKS!
GLUB 7 NEWS
SCREW YOU, DAD
BWEUP!

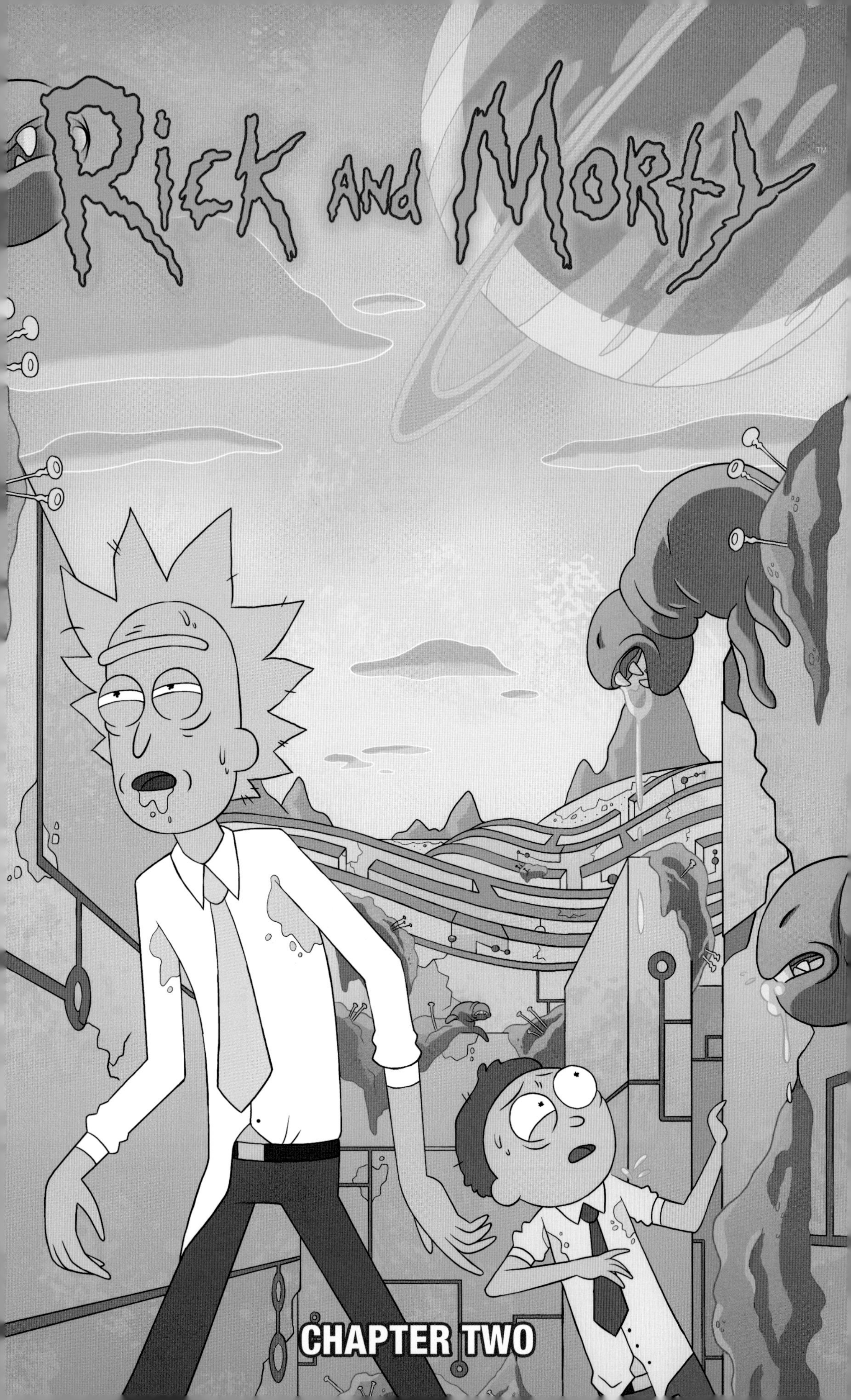
Rick and Morty™
CHAPTER TWO

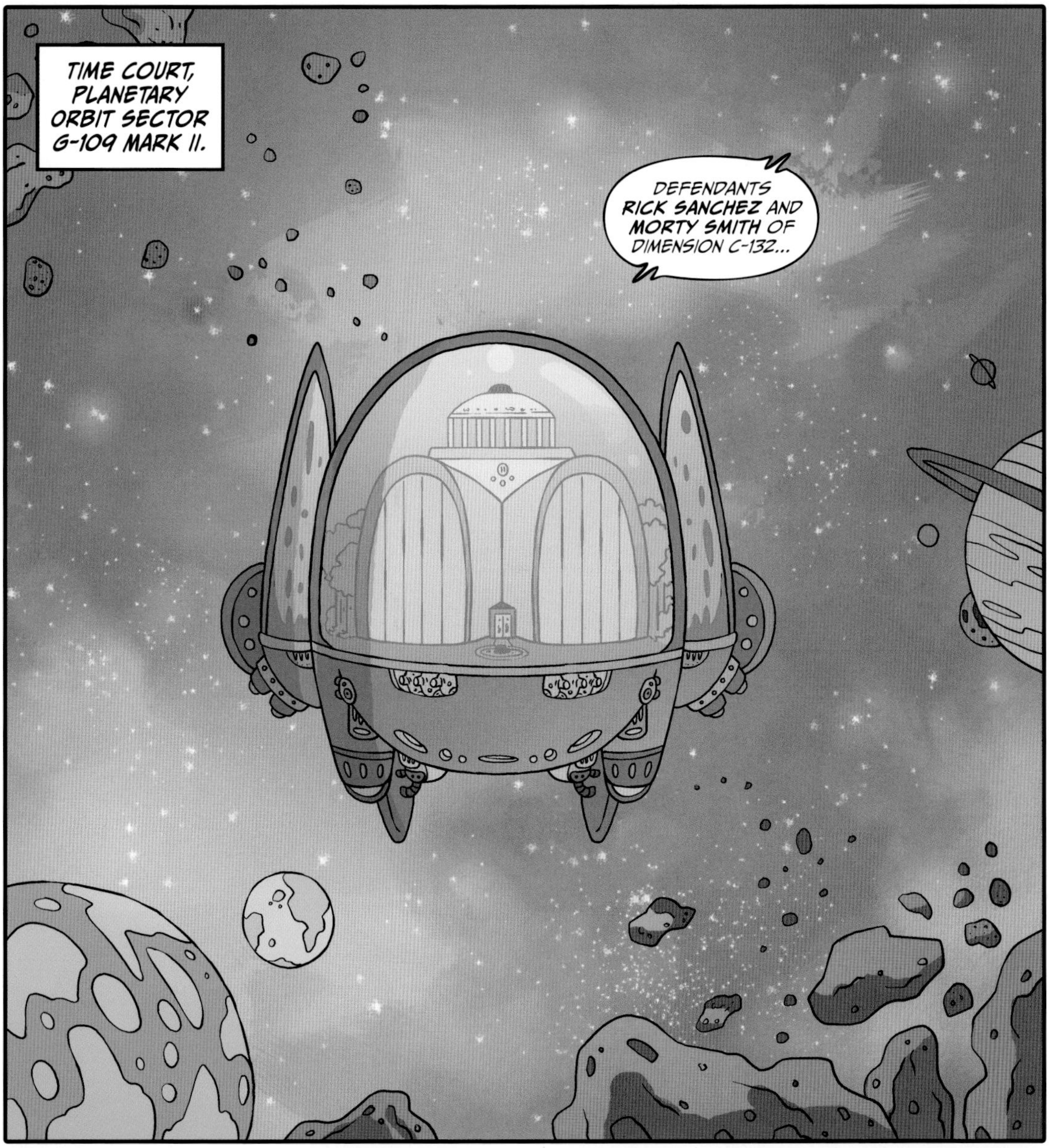
TIME COURT, PLANETARY ORBIT SECTOR G-109 MARK II.
DEFENDANTS RICK SANCHEZ AND MORTY SMITH OF DIMENSION C-132...

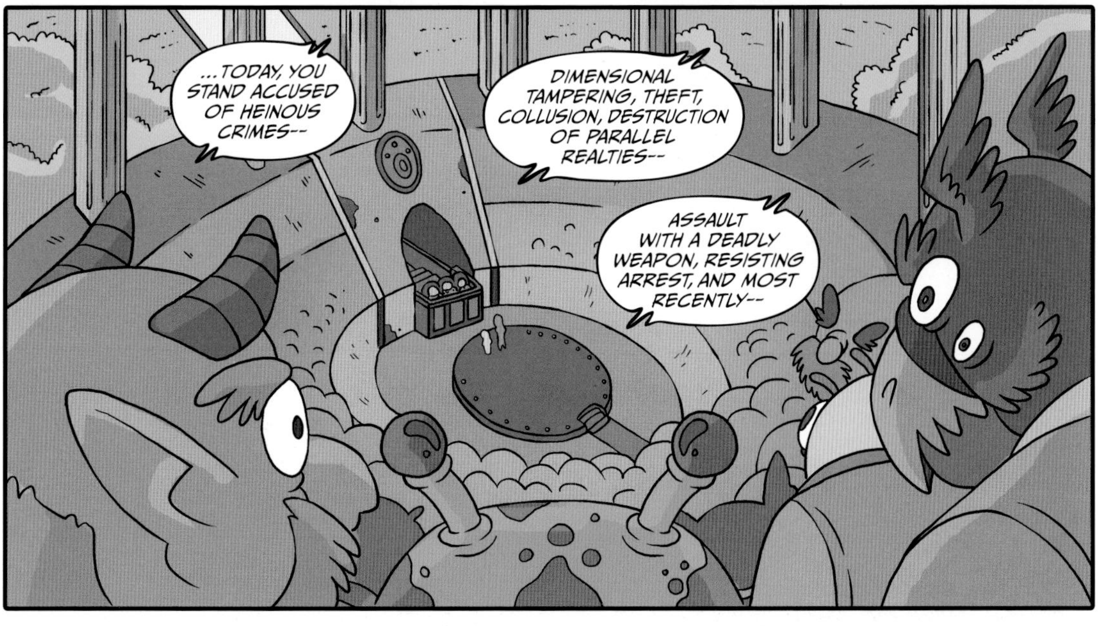
...TODAY, YOU STAND ACCUSED OF HEINOUS CRIMES--
DIMENSIONAL TAMPERING, THEFT, COLLUSION, DESTRUCTION OF PARALLEL REALTIES--
ASSAULT WITH A DEADLY WEAPON, RESISTING ARREST, AND MOST RECENTLY--

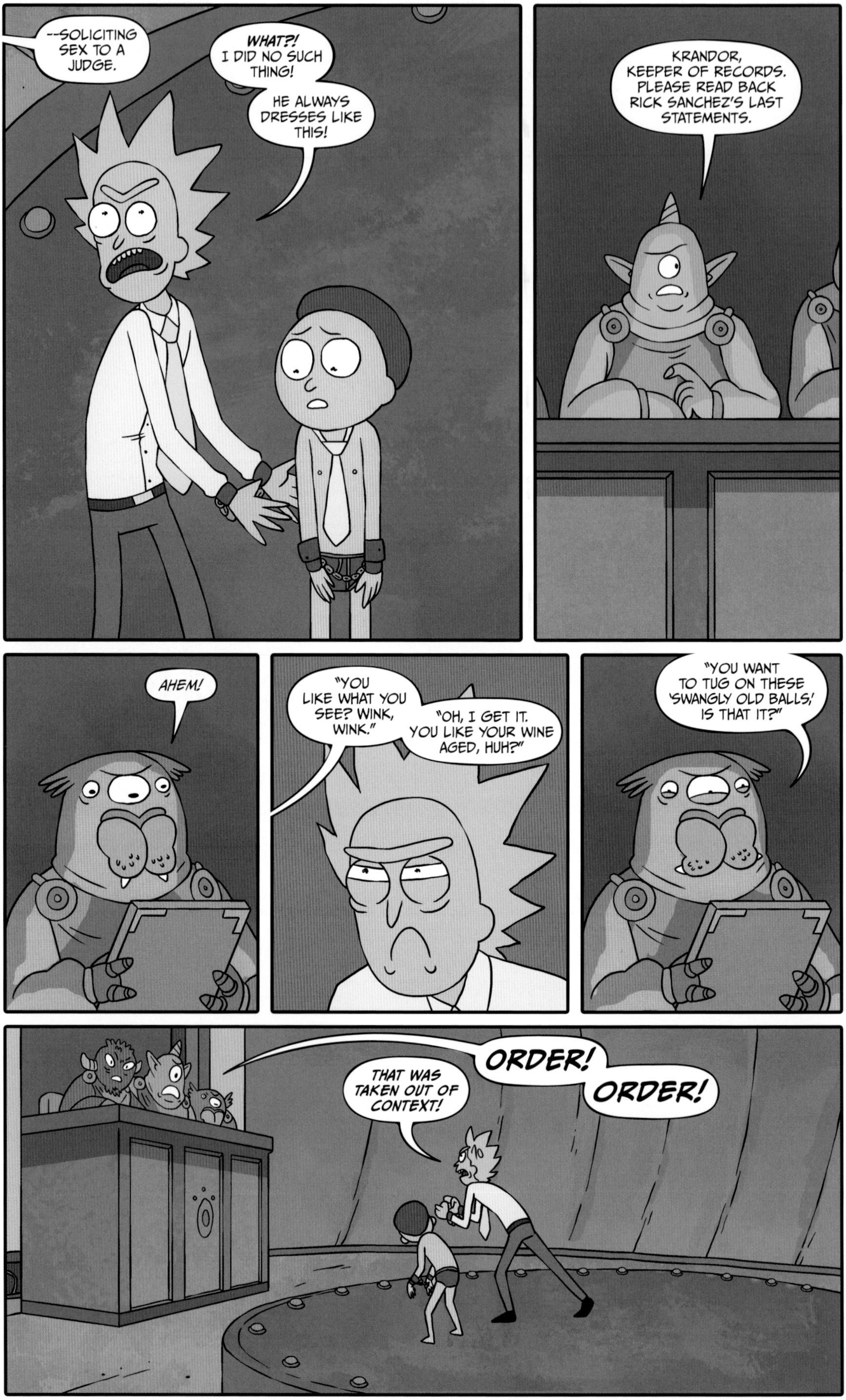
--SOLICITING SEX TO A JUDGE.
WHAT?! I DID NO SUCH THING!
HE ALWAYS DRESSES LIKE THIS!
KRANDOR, KEEPER OF RECORDS. PLEASE READ BACK RICK SANCHEZ'S LAST STATEMENTS.
AHEM!
"YOU LIKE WHAT YOU SEE? WINK, WINK."
"OH, I GET IT. YOU LIKE YOUR WINE AGED, HUH?"
"YOU WANT TO TUG ON THESE 'SWANGLY OLD BALLS,' IS THAT IT?"
ORDER! ORDER!
THAT WAS TAKEN OUT OF CONTEXT!

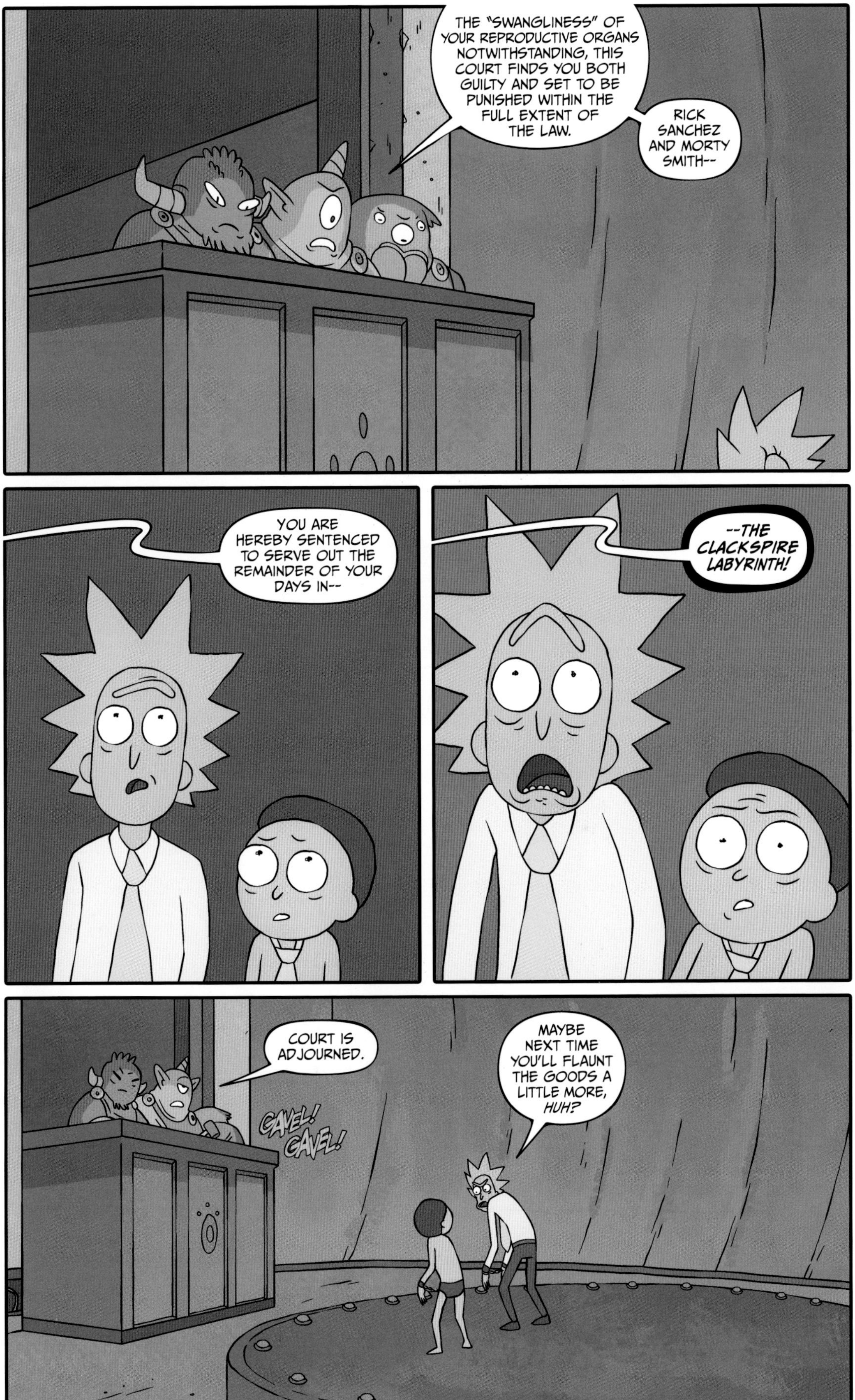
THE "SWANGLINESS" OF YOUR REPRODUCTIVE ORGANS NOTWITHSTANDING, THIS COURT FINDS YOU BOTH GUILTY AND SET TO BE PUNISHED WITHIN THE FULL EXTENT OF THE LAW.
RICK SANCHEZ AND MORTY SMITH--
YOU ARE HEREBY SENTENCED TO SERVE OUT THE REMAINDER OF YOUR DAYS IN--
--THE CLACKSPIRE LABYRINTH!
COURT IS ADJOURNED.
GAVEL! GAVEL!
MAYBE NEXT TIME YOU'LL FLAUNT THE GOODS A LITTLE MORE, HUH?

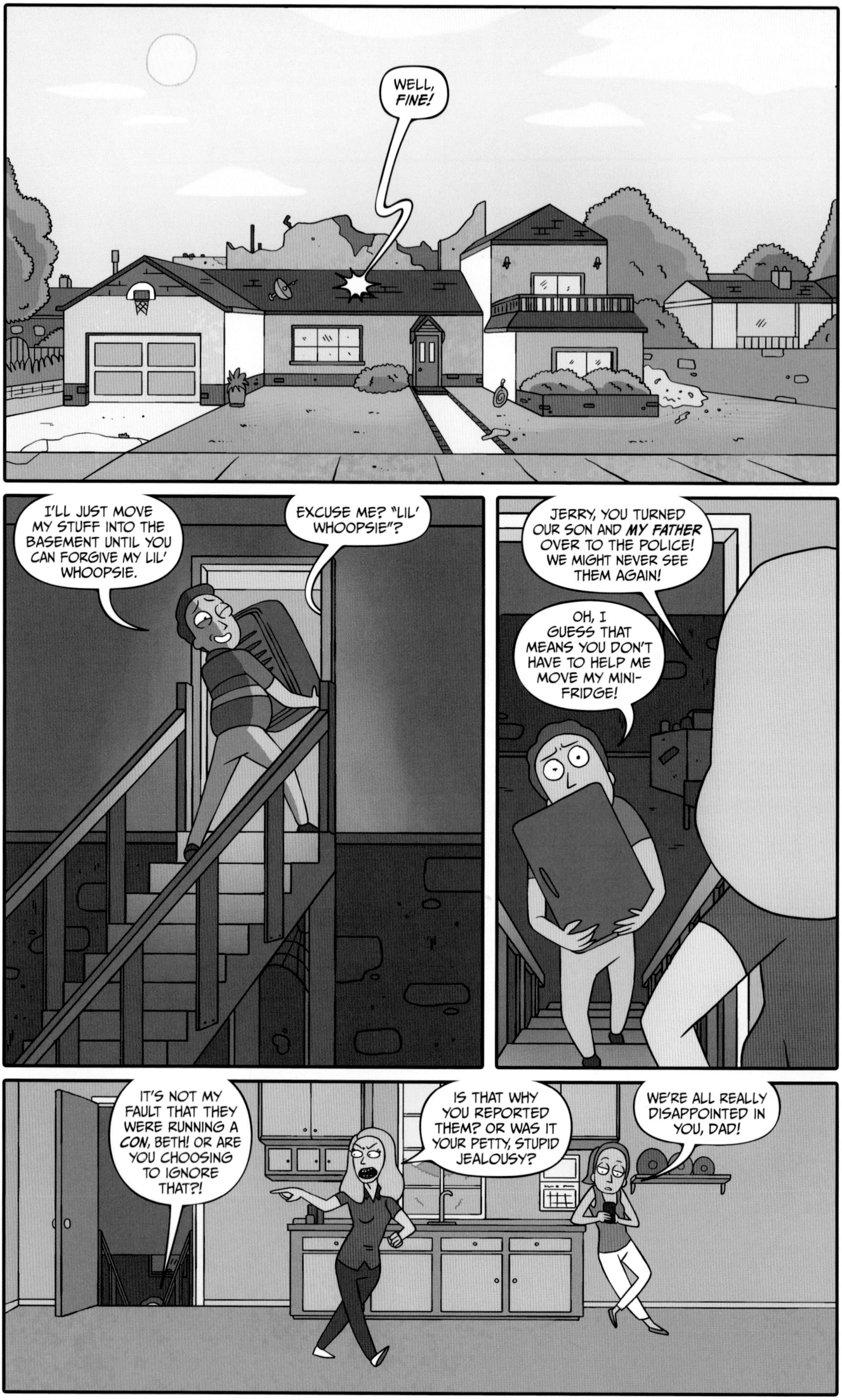
WELL, *FINE!*
I'LL JUST MOVE MY STUFF INTO THE BASEMENT UNTIL YOU CAN FORGIVE MY LIL' WHOOPSIE.
EXCUSE ME? "LIL' WHOOPSIE"?
JERRY, YOU TURNED OUR SON AND *MY FATHER* OVER TO THE POLICE! WE MIGHT NEVER SEE THEM AGAIN!
OH, I GUESS THAT MEANS YOU DON'T HAVE TO HELP ME MOVE MY MINI-FRIDGE!
IT'S NOT MY FAULT THAT THEY WERE RUNNING A *CON*, BETH! OR ARE YOU CHOOSING TO IGNORE THAT?!
IS THAT WHY YOU REPORTED THEM? OR WAS IT YOUR PETTY, STUPID JEALOUSY?
WE'RE ALL REALLY DISAPPOINTED IN YOU, DAD!

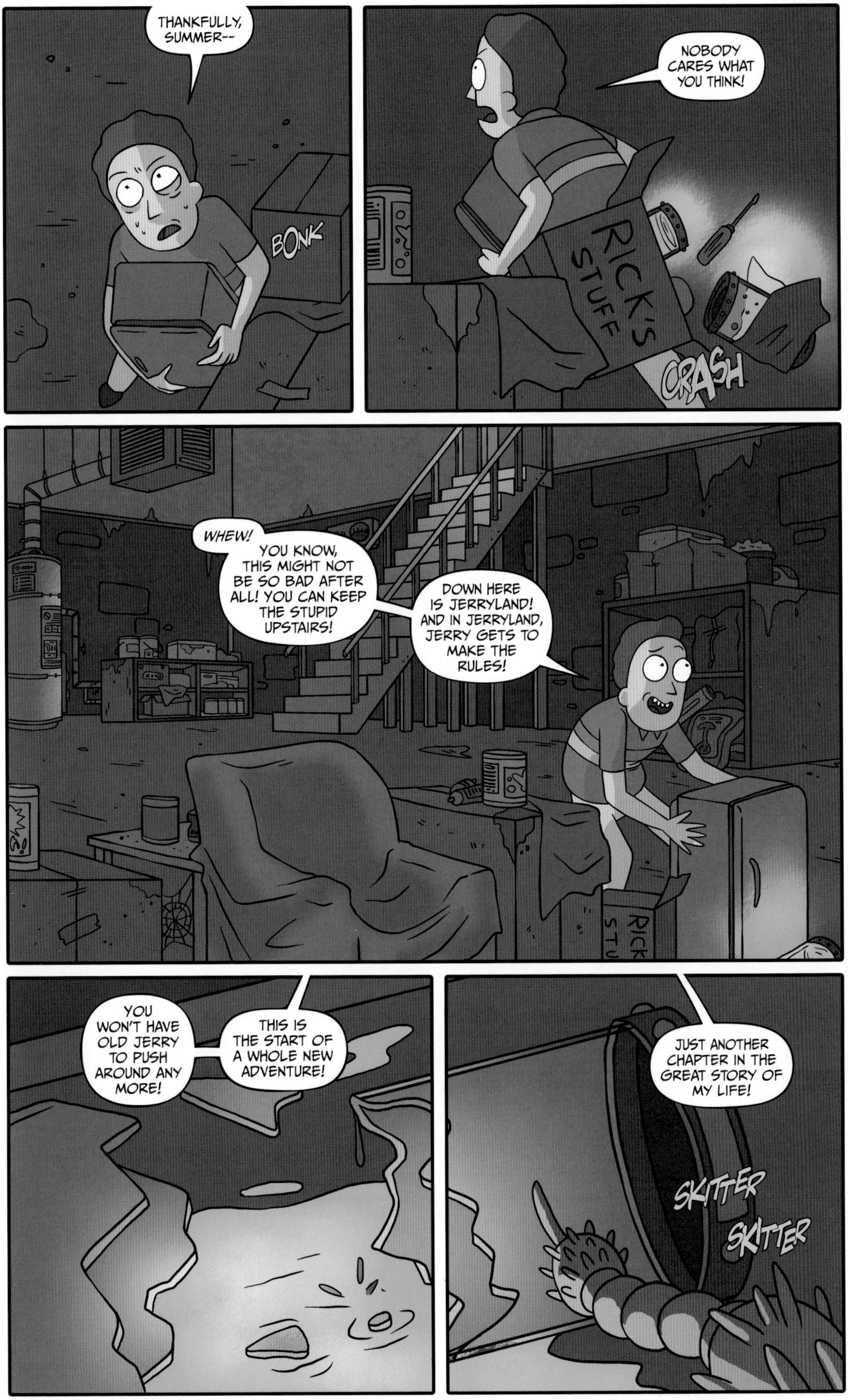
THANKFULLY, SUMMER--
BONK
NOBODY CARES WHAT YOU THINK!
RICK'S STUFF
CRASH
WHEW!
YOU KNOW, THIS MIGHT NOT BE SO BAD AFTER ALL! YOU CAN KEEP THE STUPID UPSTAIRS!
DOWN HERE IS JERRYLAND! AND IN JERRYLAND, JERRY GETS TO MAKE THE RULES!
YOU WON'T HAVE OLD JERRY TO PUSH AROUND ANY MORE!
THIS IS THE START OF A WHOLE NEW ADVENTURE!
JUST ANOTHER CHAPTER IN THE GREAT STORY OF MY LIFE!
SKITTER
SKITTER

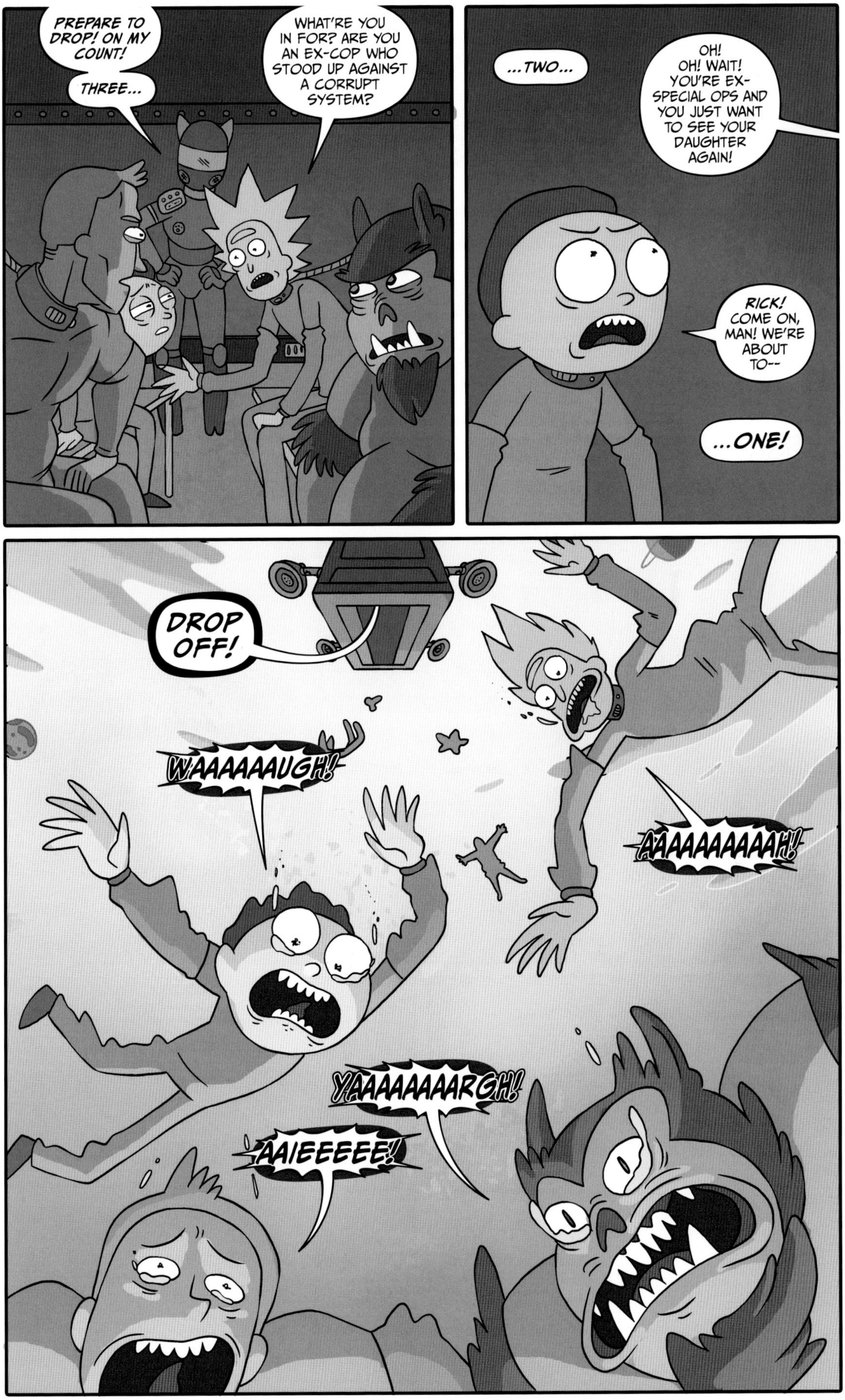
PREPARE TO DROP! ON MY COUNT!
THREE...
WHAT'RE YOU IN FOR? ARE YOU AN EX-COP WHO STOOD UP AGAINST A CORRUPT SYSTEM?
...TWO...
OH! OH! WAIT! YOU'RE EX-SPECIAL OPS AND YOU JUST WANT TO SEE YOUR DAUGHTER AGAIN!
RICK! COME ON, MAN! WE'RE ABOUT TO--
...ONE!
DROP OFF!
WAAAAAAUGH!
AAAAAAAAAAH!
YAAAAAAAARGH!
AAIEEEEEE!

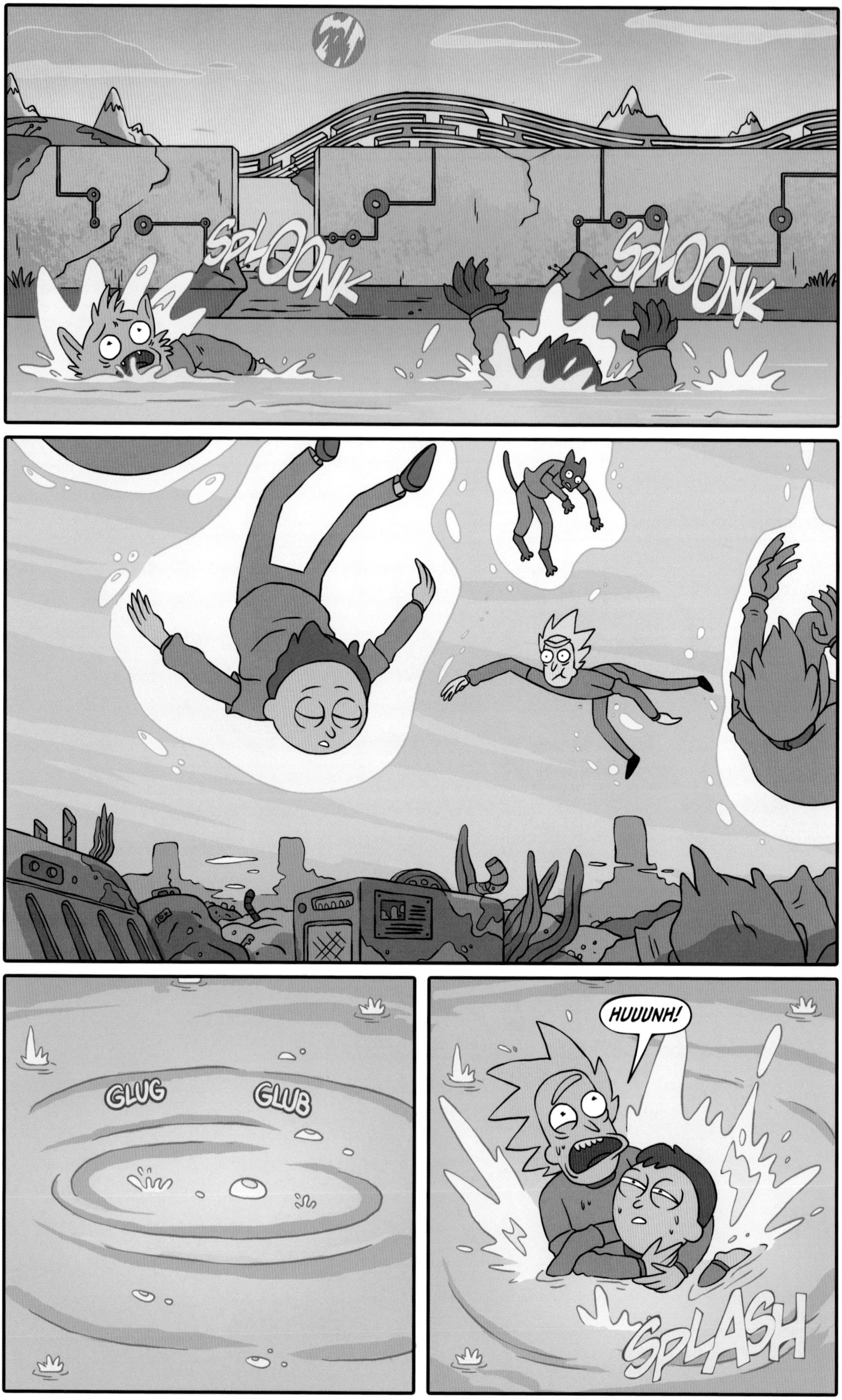
SPLOONK
SPLOONK
GLUG
GLUB
HUUUNH!
SPLASH

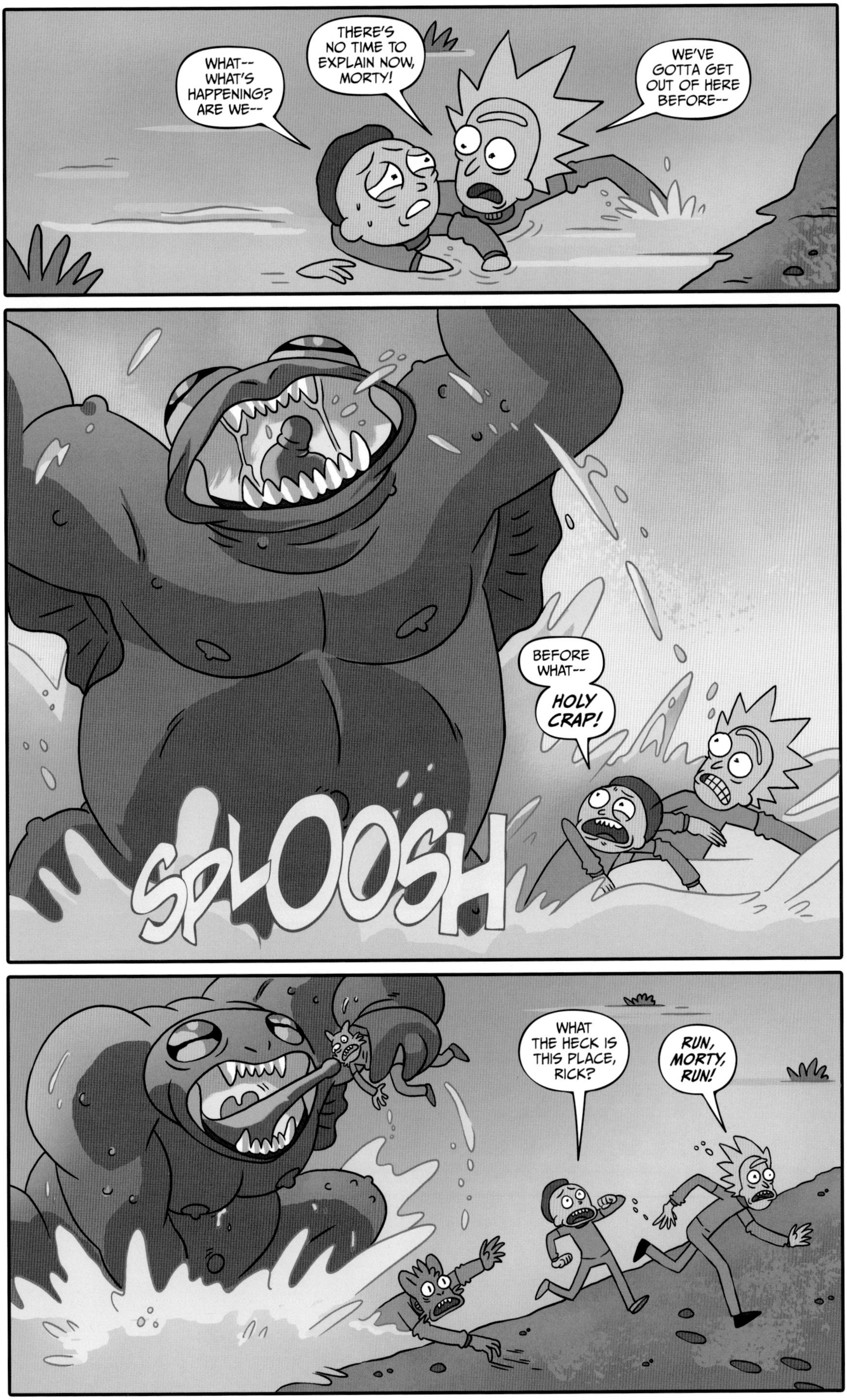
WHAT-- WHAT'S HAPPENING? ARE WE--
THERE'S NO TIME TO EXPLAIN NOW, MORTY!
WE'VE GOTTA GET OUT OF HERE BEFORE--
BEFORE WHAT-- HOLY CRAP!
SPLOOSH
WHAT THE HECK IS THIS PLACE, RICK?
RUN, MORTY, RUN!

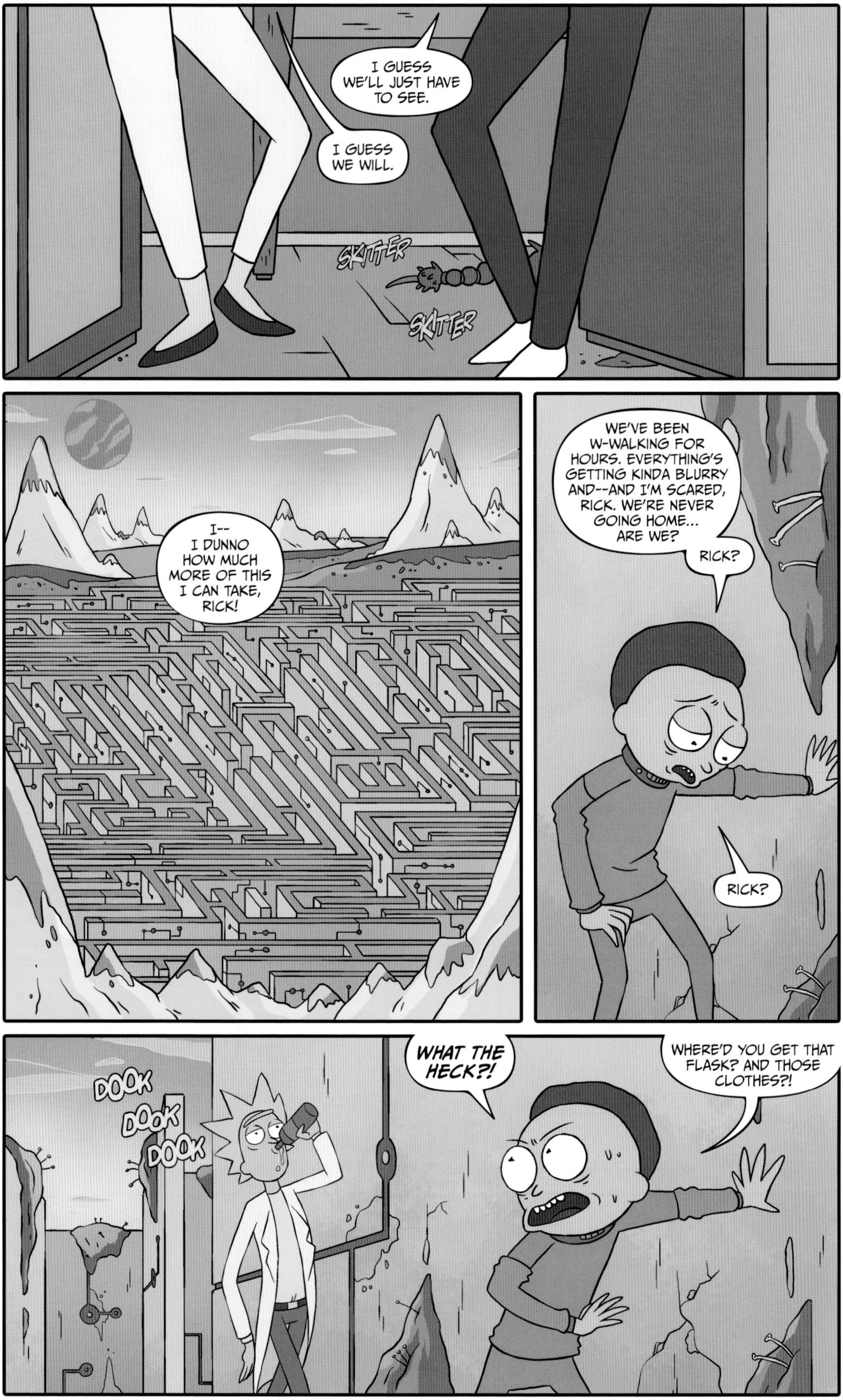

I GUESS WE'LL JUST HAVE TO SEE.
I GUESS WE WILL.
SKITTER
SKITTER
I-- I DUNNO HOW MUCH MORE OF THIS I CAN TAKE, RICK!
WE'VE BEEN W-WALKING FOR HOURS. EVERYTHING'S GETTING KINDA BLURRY AND--AND I'M SCARED, RICK. WE'RE NEVER GOING HOME... ARE WE?
RICK?
RICK?
DOOK
DOOK
DOOK
WHAT THE HECK?!
WHERE'D YOU GET THAT FLASK? AND THOSE CLOTHES?!

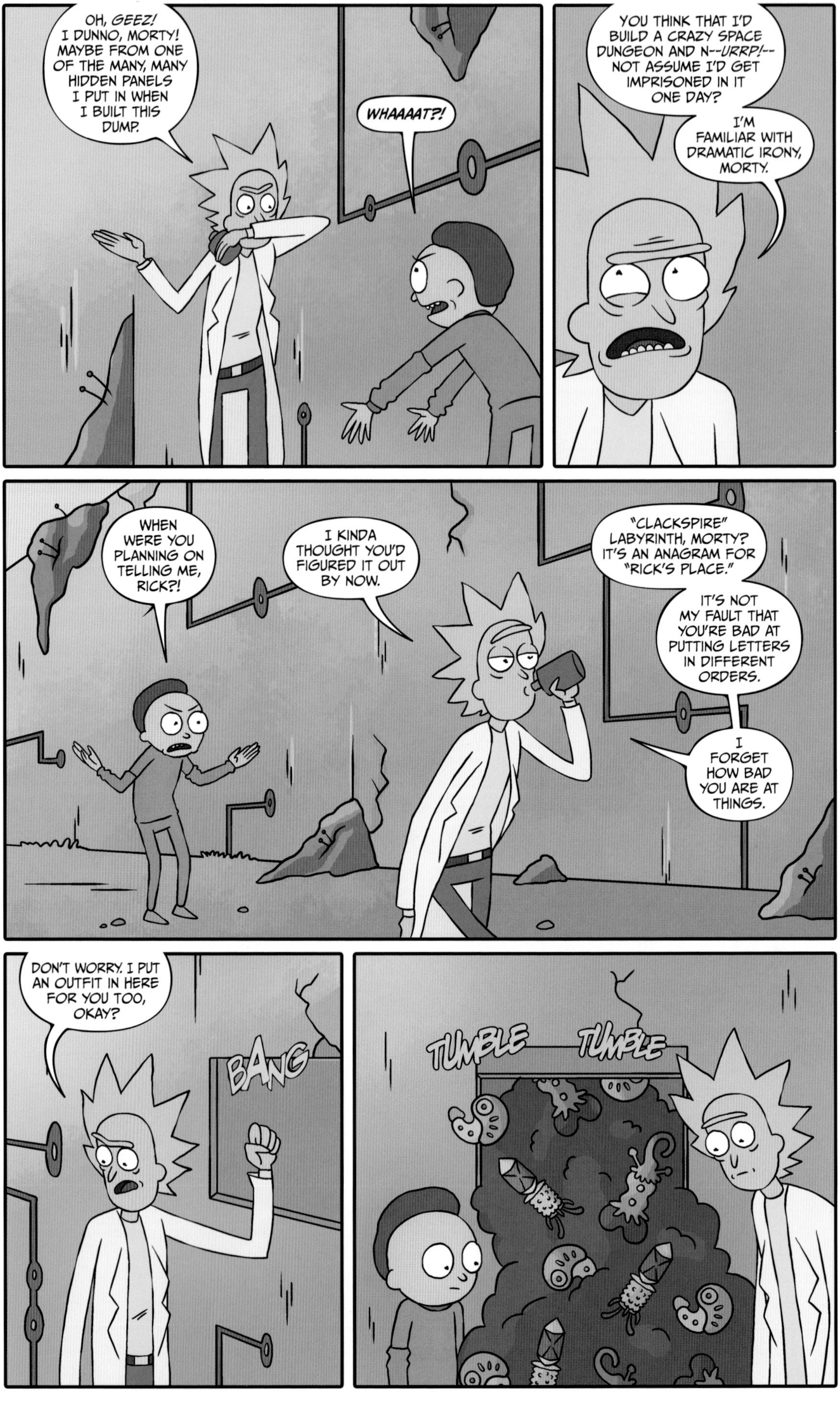
OH, GEEZ! I DUNNO, MORTY! MAYBE FROM ONE OF THE MANY, MANY HIDDEN PANELS I PUT IN WHEN I BUILT THIS DUMP.
WHAAAAT?!
YOU THINK THAT I'D BUILD A CRAZY SPACE DUNGEON AND N--URRP!-- NOT ASSUME I'D GET IMPRISONED IN IT ONE DAY?
I'M FAMILIAR WITH DRAMATIC IRONY, MORTY.
WHEN WERE YOU PLANNING ON TELLING ME, RICK?!
I KINDA THOUGHT YOU'D FIGURED IT OUT BY NOW.
"CLACKSPIRE" LABYRINTH, MORTY? IT'S AN ANAGRAM FOR "RICK'S PLACE."
IT'S NOT MY FAULT THAT YOU'RE BAD AT PUTTING LETTERS IN DIFFERENT ORDERS.
I FORGET HOW BAD YOU ARE AT THINGS.
DON'T WORRY. I PUT AN OUTFIT IN HERE FOR YOU TOO, OKAY?
BANG
TUMBLE TUMBLE

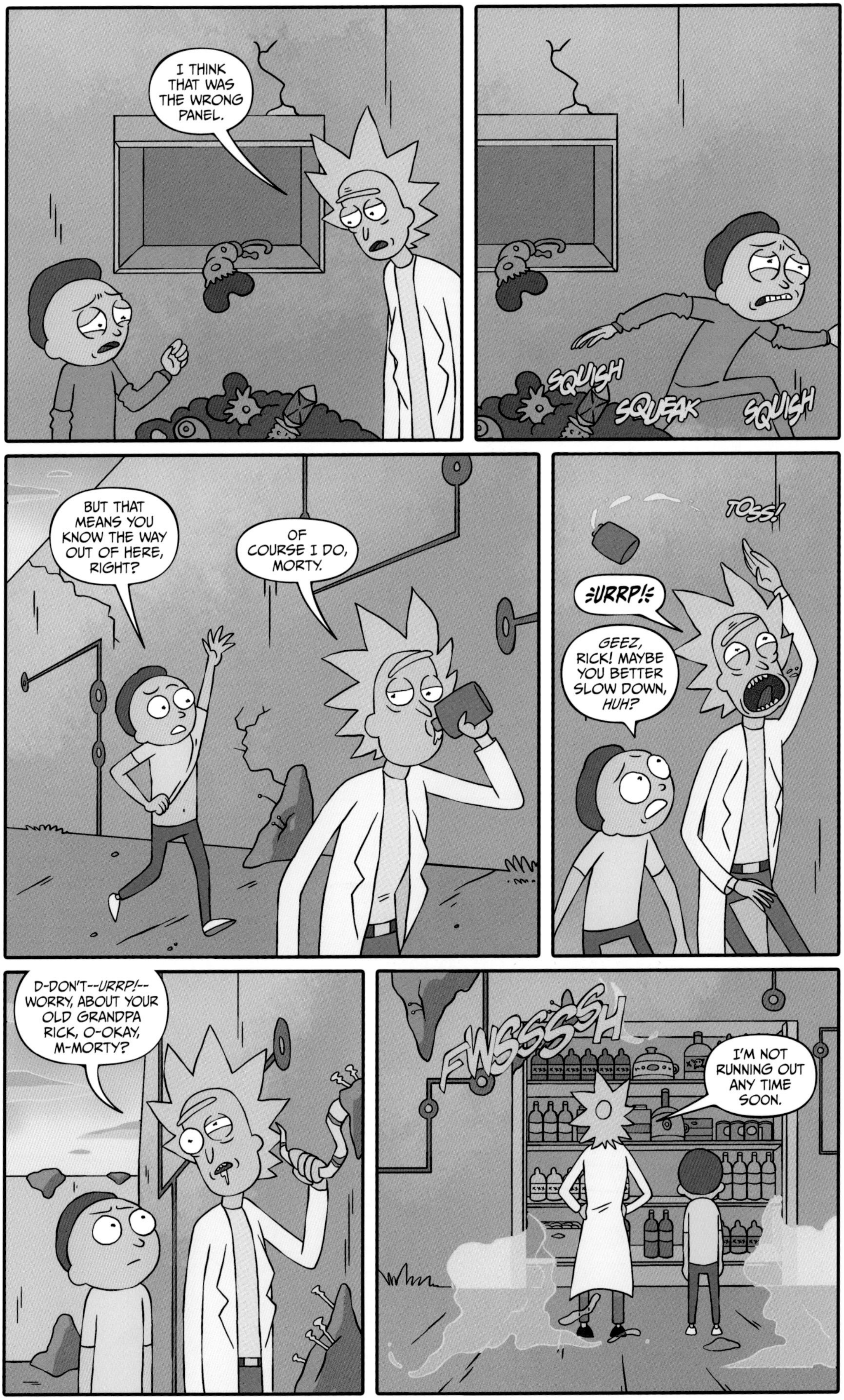
I THINK THAT WAS THE WRONG PANEL.
SQUISH
SQUEAK
SQUISH
BUT THAT MEANS YOU KNOW THE WAY OUT OF HERE, RIGHT?
OF COURSE I DO, MORTY.
TOSS!
URRP!
GEEZ, RICK! MAYBE YOU BETTER SLOW DOWN, HUH?
D-DON'T--URRP!--WORRY, ABOUT YOUR OLD GRANDPA RICK, O-OKAY, M-MORTY?
FWSSSSH
I'M NOT RUNNING OUT ANY TIME SOON.

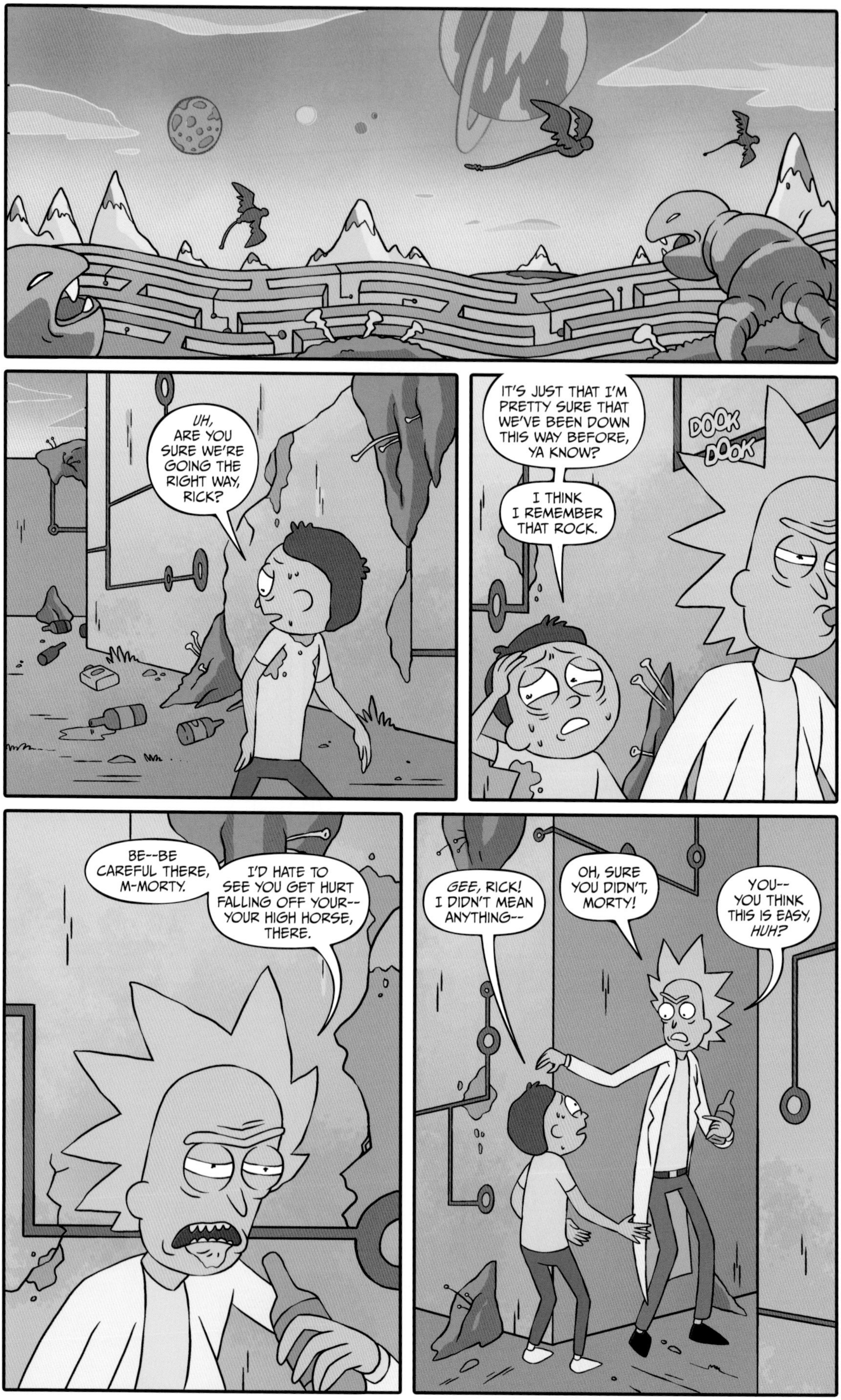
UH, ARE YOU SURE WE'RE GOING THE RIGHT WAY, RICK?
IT'S JUST THAT I'M PRETTY SURE THAT WE'VE BEEN DOWN THIS WAY BEFORE, YA KNOW?
DOOK DOOK
I THINK I REMEMBER THAT ROCK.
BE--BE CAREFUL THERE, M-MORTY.
I'D HATE TO SEE YOU GET HURT FALLING OFF YOUR-- YOUR HIGH HORSE, THERE.
GEE, RICK! I DIDN'T MEAN ANYTHING--
OH, SURE YOU DIDN'T, MORTY!
YOU-- YOU THINK THIS IS EASY, HUH?

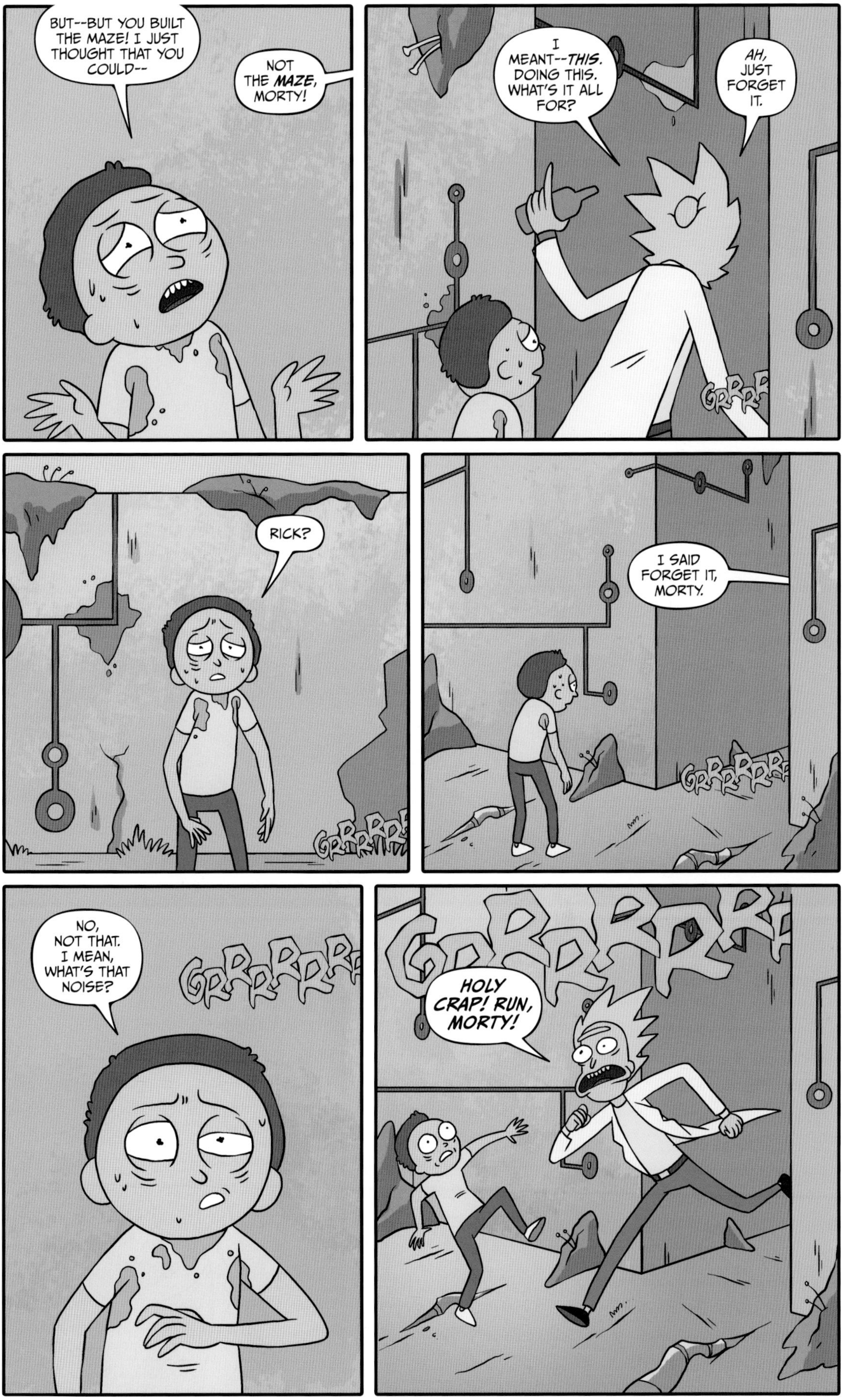
BUT--BUT YOU BUILT THE MAZE! I JUST THOUGHT THAT YOU COULD--
NOT THE *MAZE*, MORTY!
I MEANT--*THIS*. DOING THIS. WHAT'S IT ALL FOR?
AH, JUST FORGET IT.
GRRRR
RICK?
GRRRRR
I SAID FORGET IT, MORTY.
GRRRRRR
NO, NOT THAT. I MEAN, WHAT'S THAT NOISE?
GRRRRRR
GRRRRRR
HOLY CRAP! RUN, MORTY!

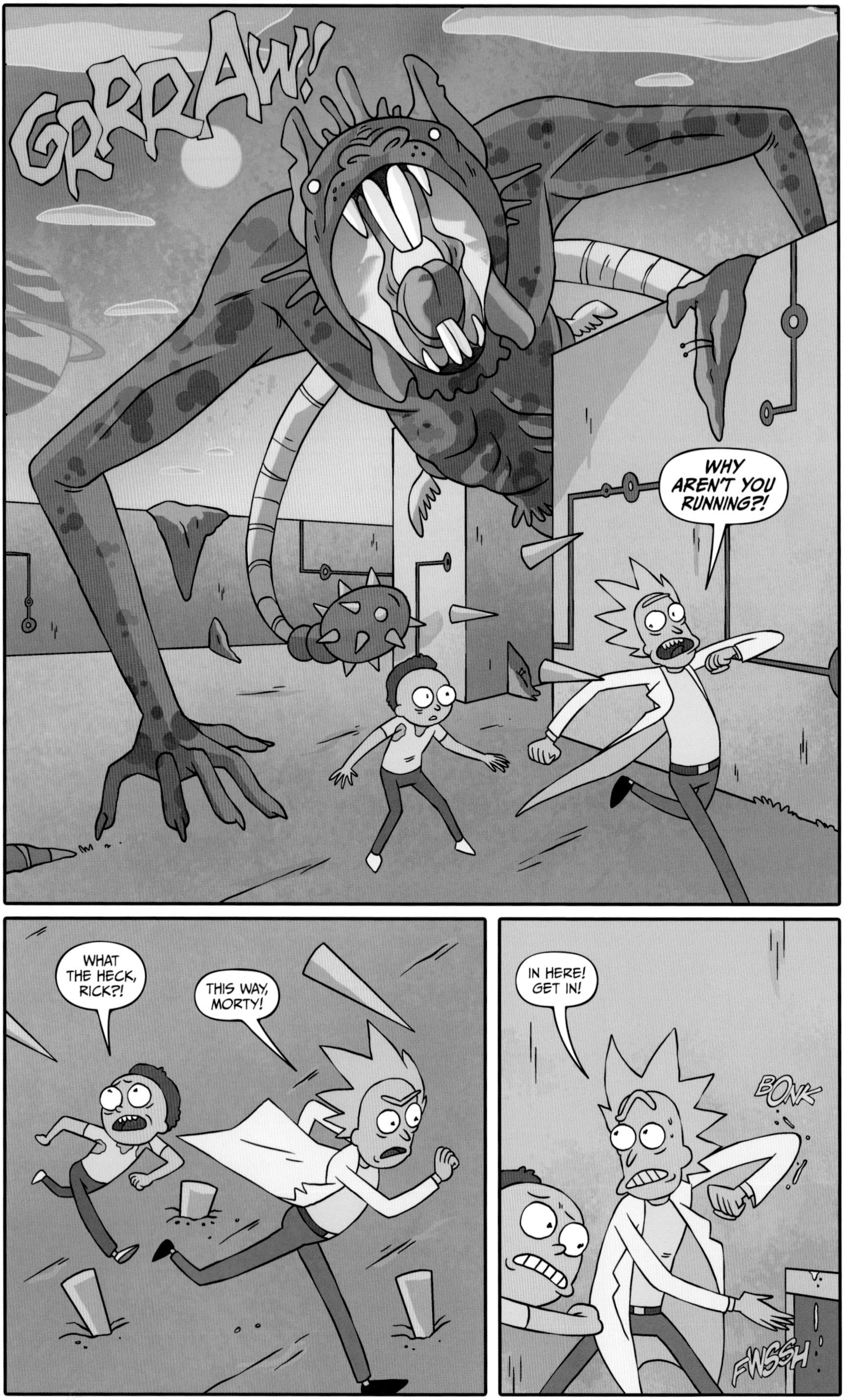
GRRRAW!!
WHY AREN'T YOU RUNNING?!
WHAT THE HECK, RICK?!
THIS WAY, MORTY!
IN HERE! GET IN!
BONK
FWSSH

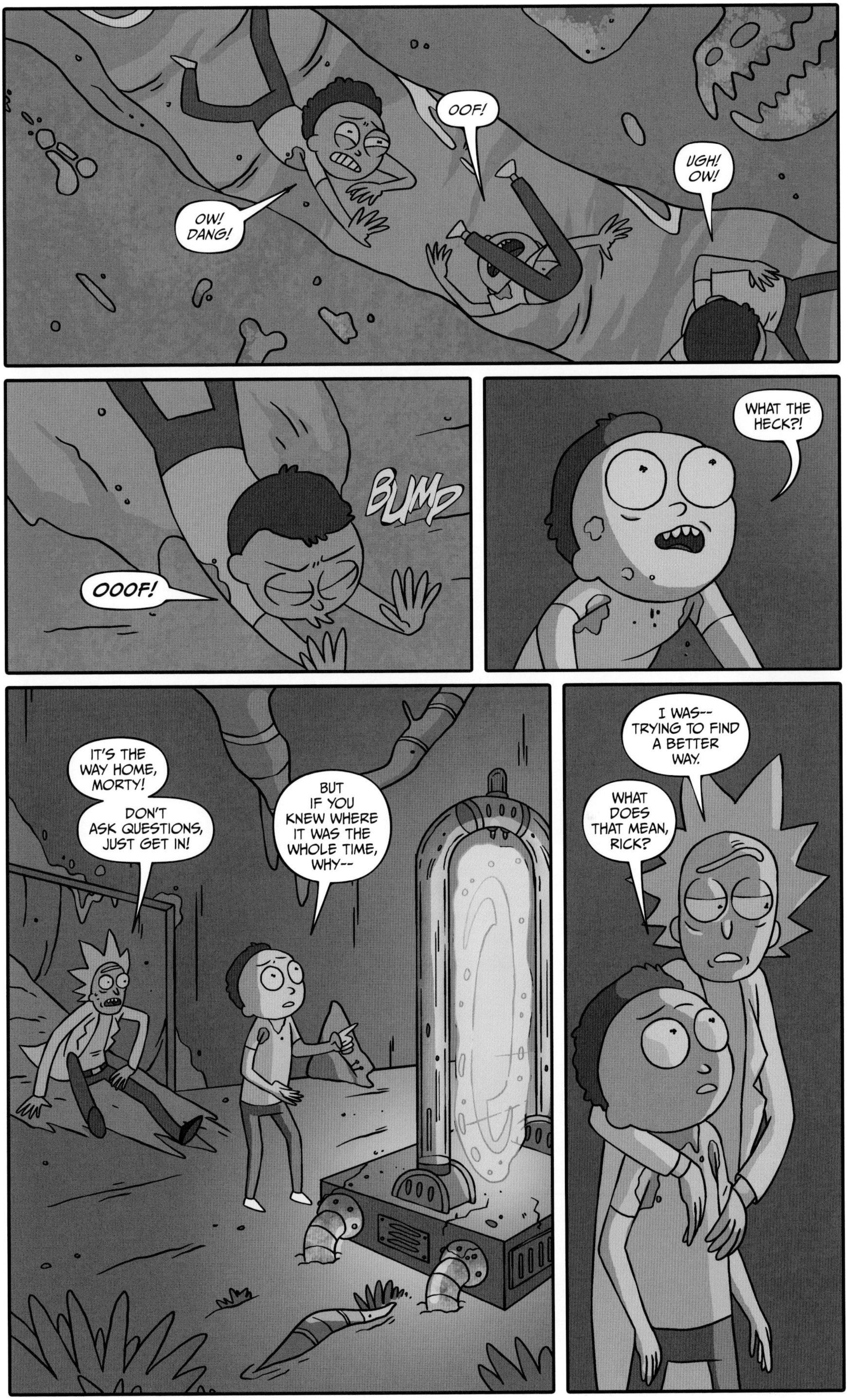

OW! DANG!
OOF!
UGH! OW!
OOOF!
BUMP
WHAT THE HECK?!
IT'S THE WAY HOME, MORTY!
DON'T ASK QUESTIONS, JUST GET IN!
BUT IF YOU KNEW WHERE IT WAS THE WHOLE TIME, WHY--
WHAT DOES THAT MEAN, RICK?
I WAS-- TRYING TO FIND A BETTER WAY.

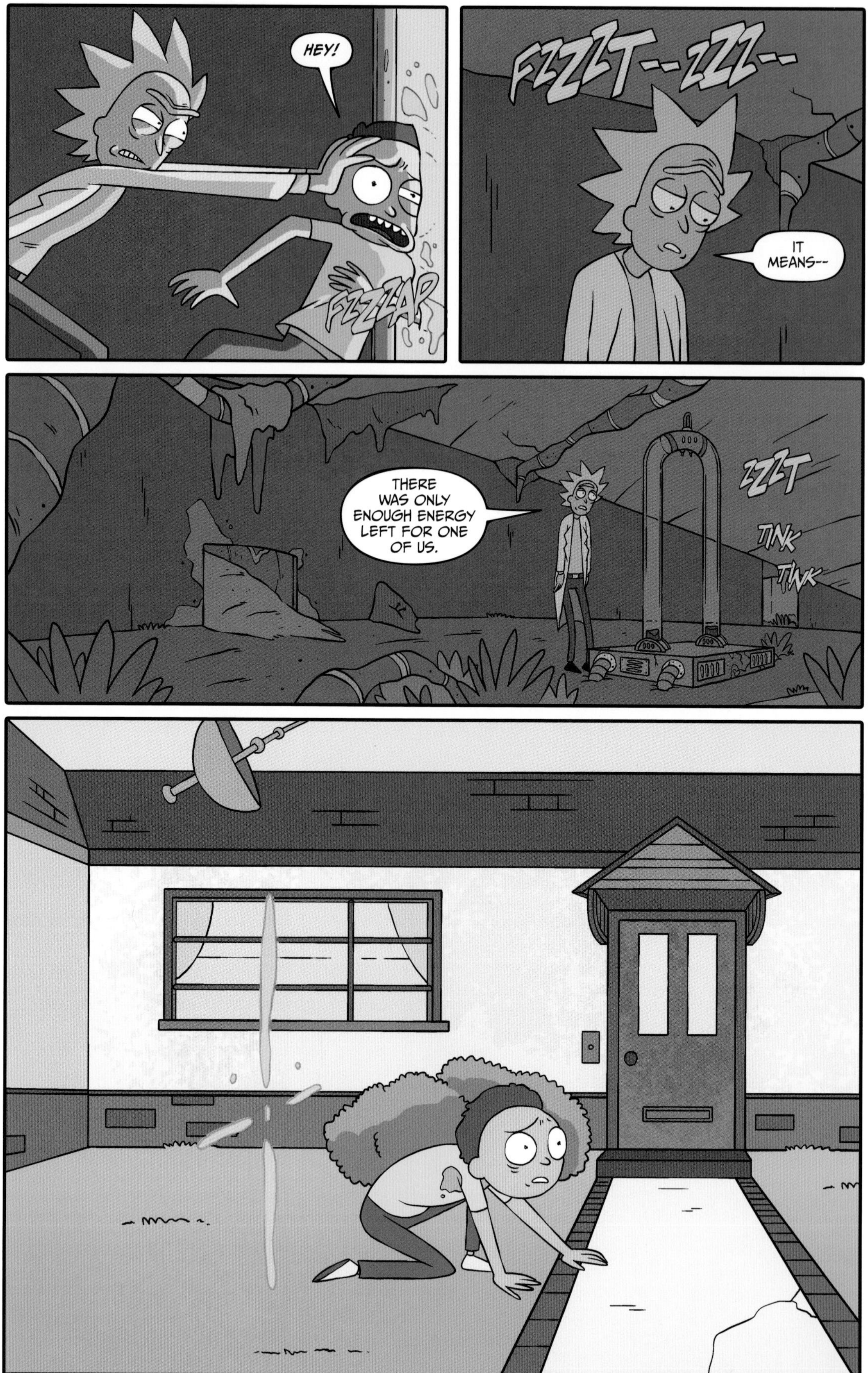
HEY!
FZZZAP
FZZZT--ZZZ--
IT MEANS--
THERE WAS ONLY ENOUGH ENERGY LEFT FOR ONE OF US.
ZZZT
TINK
TINK

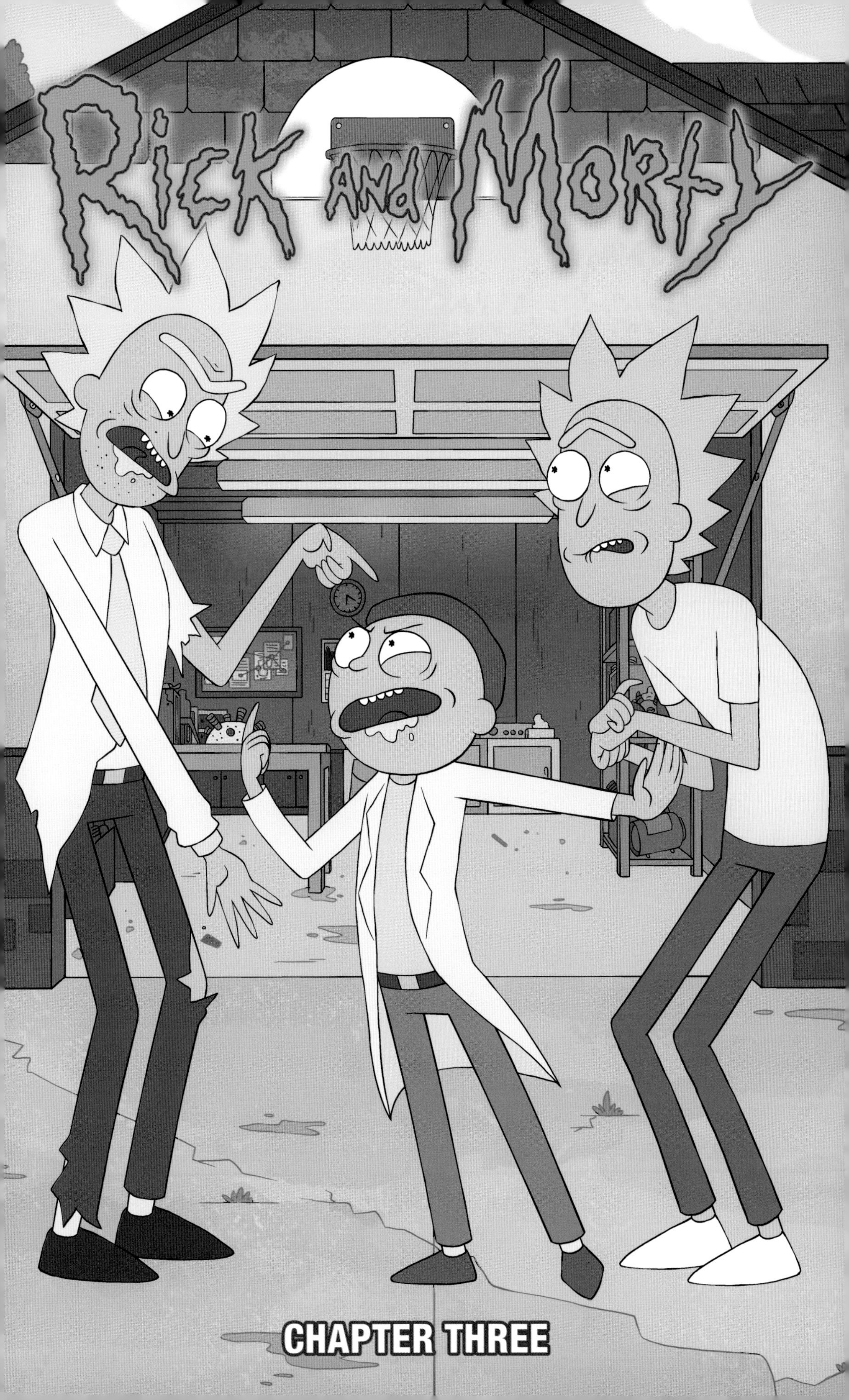
Rick and Morty
CHAPTER THREE

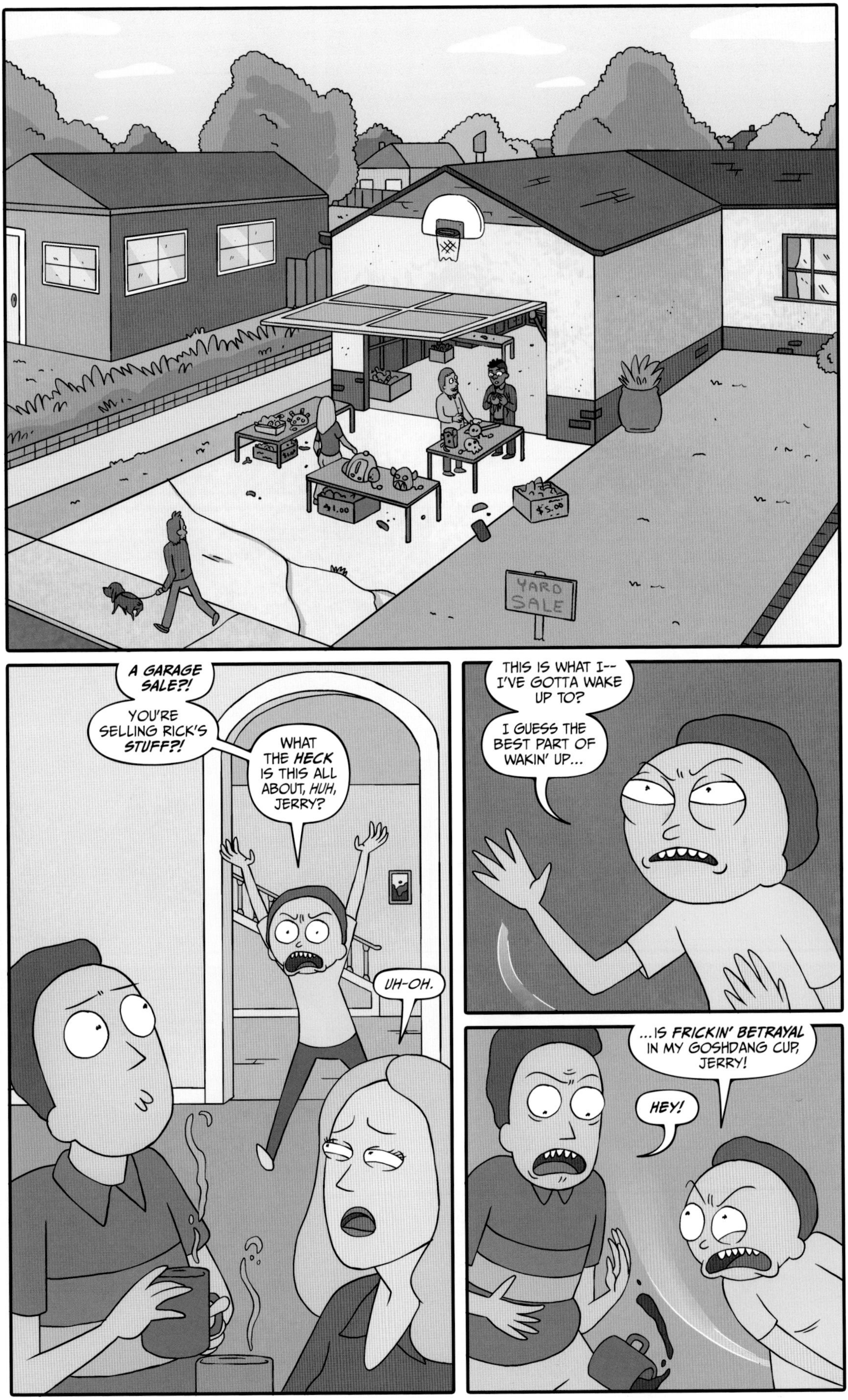
YARD SALE
$1.00
$5.00
A GARAGE SALE?!
YOU'RE SELLING RICK'S STUFF?!
WHAT THE HECK IS THIS ALL ABOUT, HUH, JERRY?
UH-OH.
THIS IS WHAT I-- I'VE GOTTA WAKE UP TO?
I GUESS THE BEST PART OF WAKIN' UP...
...IS FRICKIN' BETRAYAL IN MY GOSHDANG CUP, JERRY!
HEY!

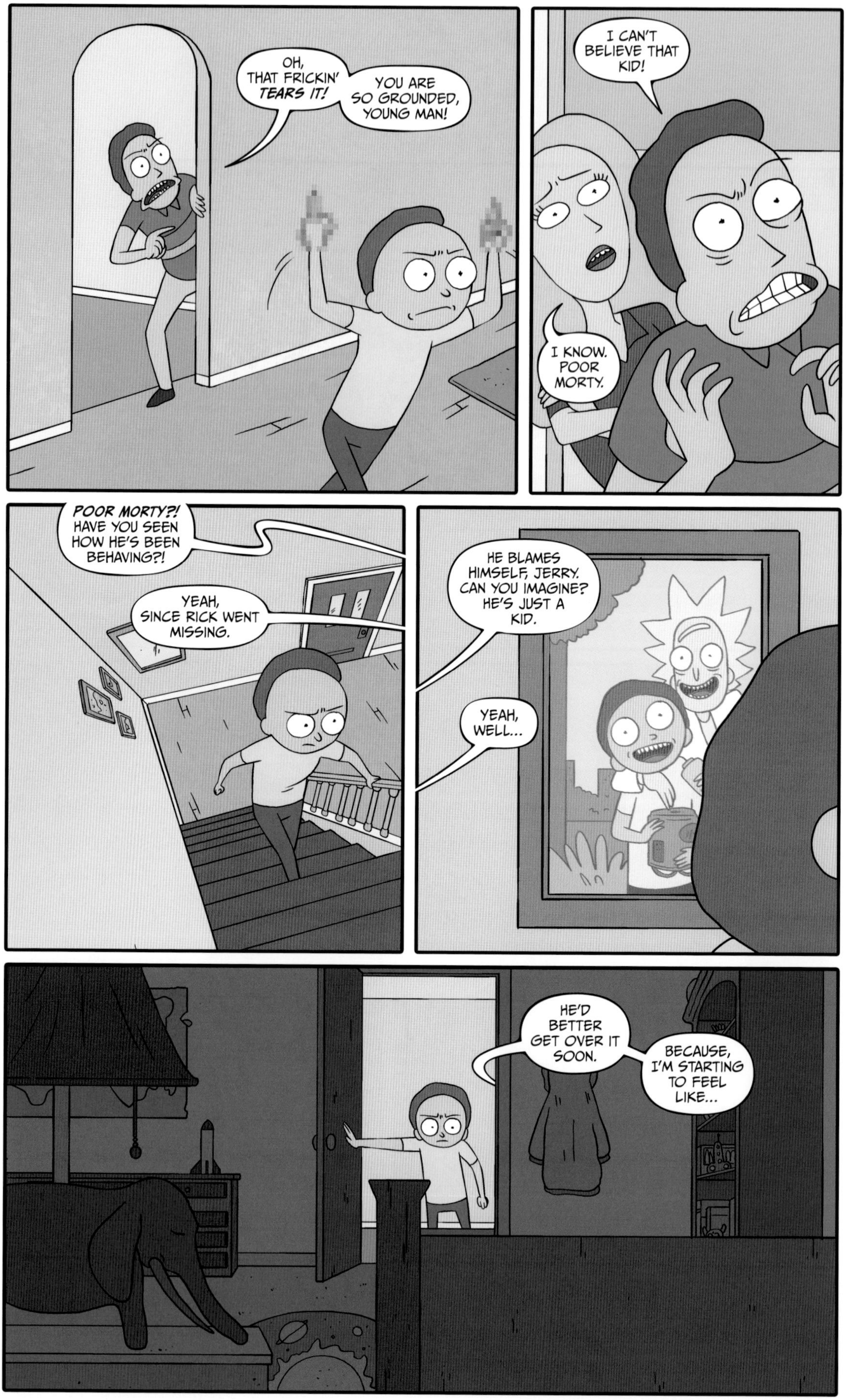
OH, THAT FRICKIN' *TEARS IT!*
YOU ARE SO GROUNDED, YOUNG MAN!
I CAN'T BELIEVE THAT KID!
I KNOW. POOR MORTY.
POOR MORTY?! HAVE YOU SEEN HOW HE'S BEEN BEHAVING?!
YEAH, SINCE RICK WENT MISSING.
HE BLAMES HIMSELF, JERRY. CAN YOU IMAGINE? HE'S JUST A KID.
YEAH, WELL...
HE'D BETTER GET OVER IT SOON.
BECAUSE, I'M STARTING TO FEEL LIKE...

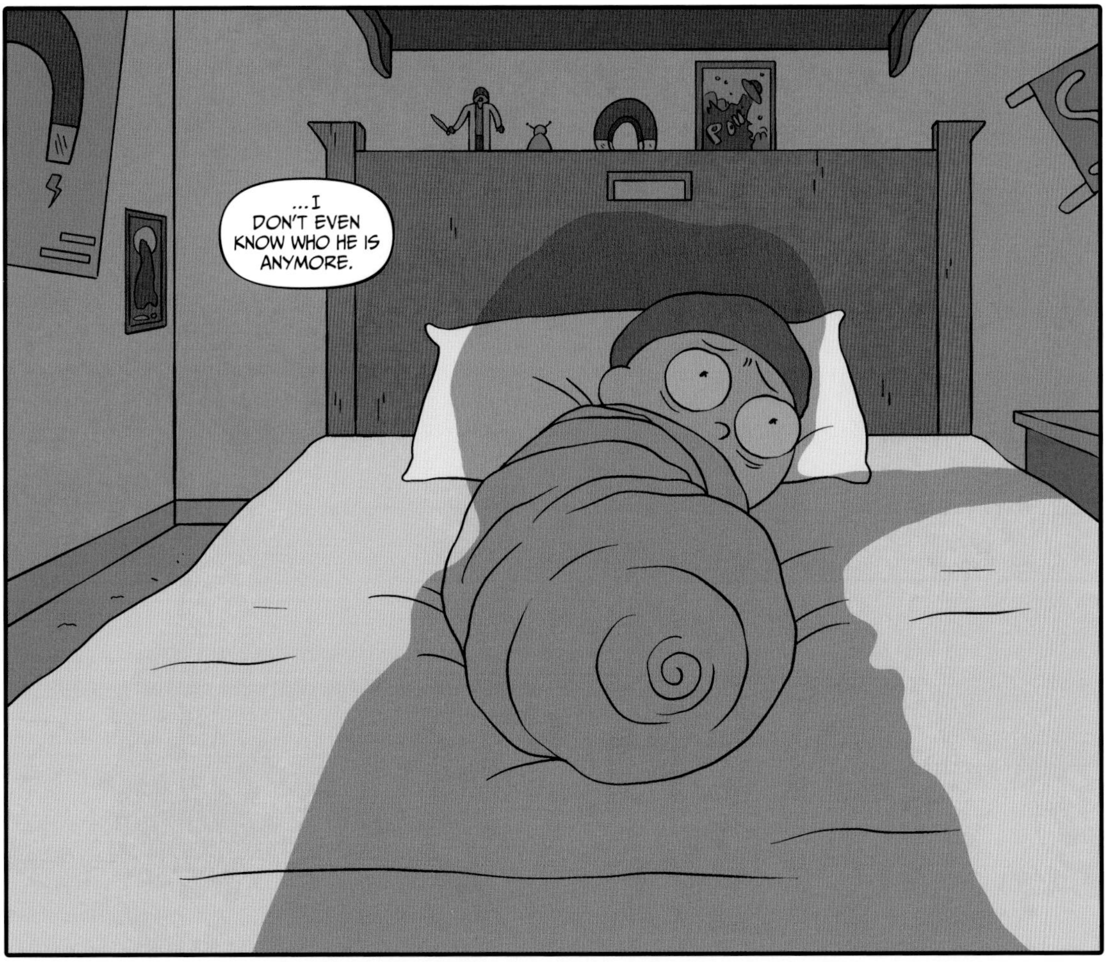
...I DON'T EVEN KNOW WHO HE IS ANYMORE.

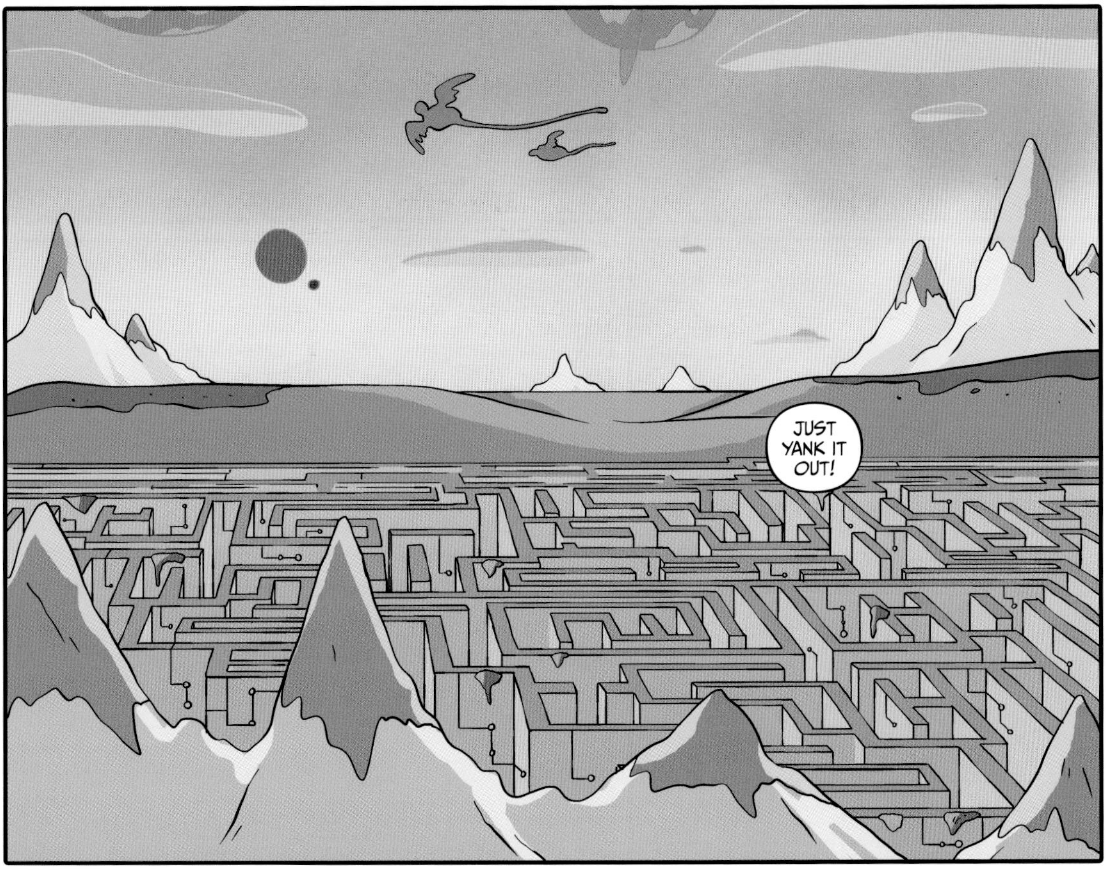
JUST YANK IT OUT!

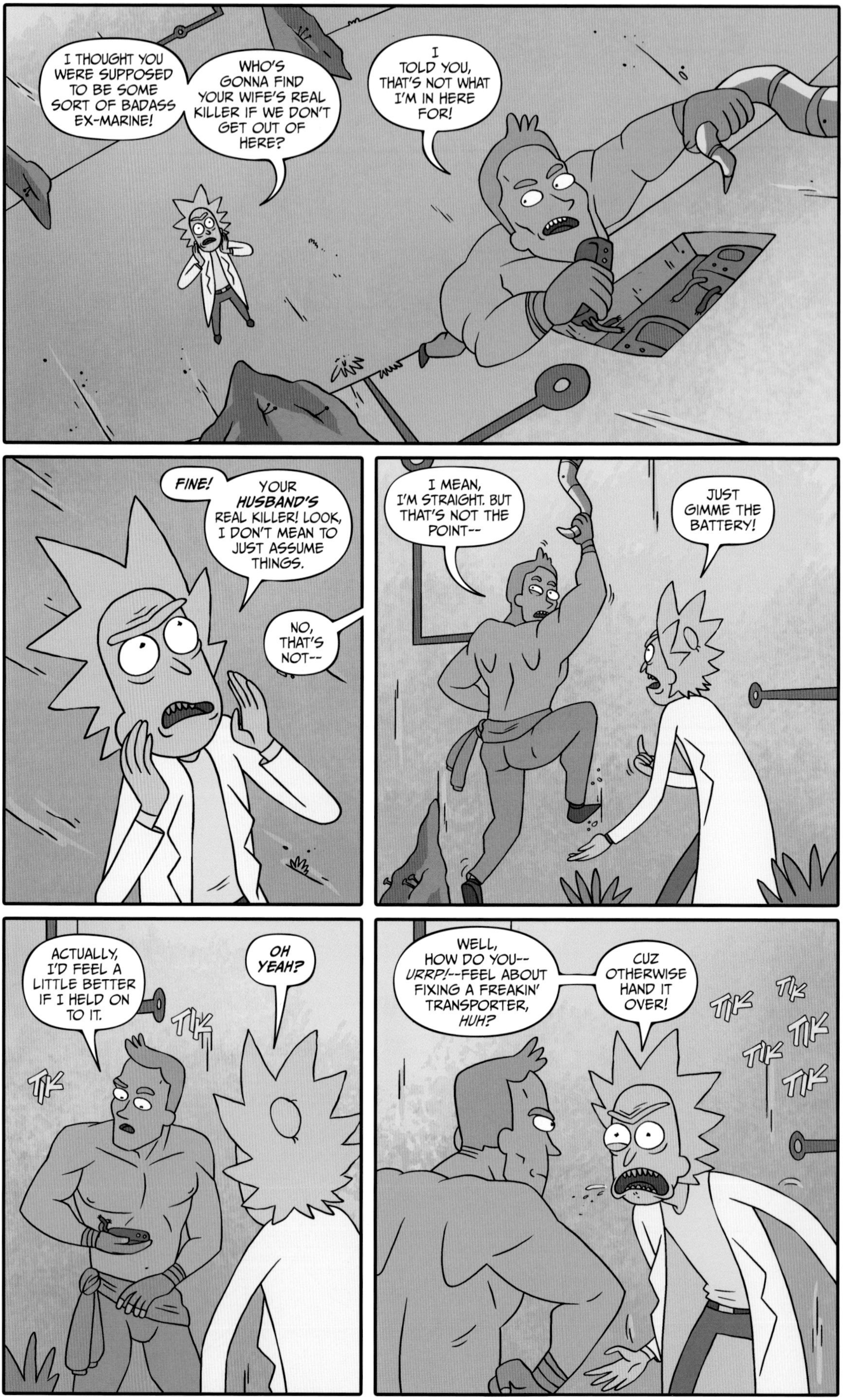

I THOUGHT YOU WERE SUPPOSED TO BE SOME SORT OF BADASS EX-MARINE!
WHO'S GONNA FIND YOUR WIFE'S REAL KILLER IF WE DON'T GET OUT OF HERE?
I TOLD YOU, THAT'S NOT WHAT I'M IN HERE FOR!
FINE!
YOUR *HUSBAND'S* REAL KILLER! LOOK, I DON'T MEAN TO JUST ASSUME THINGS.
NO, THAT'S NOT--
I MEAN, I'M STRAIGHT. BUT THAT'S NOT THE POINT--
JUST GIMME THE BATTERY!
ACTUALLY, I'D FEEL A LITTLE BETTER IF I HELD ON TO IT.
TIK
TIK
OH YEAH?
WELL, HOW DO YOU-- *URRP!*--FEEL ABOUT FIXING A FREAKIN' TRANSPORTER, *HUH?*
CUZ OTHERWISE HAND IT OVER!
TIK
TIK
TIK
TIK
TIK
TIK

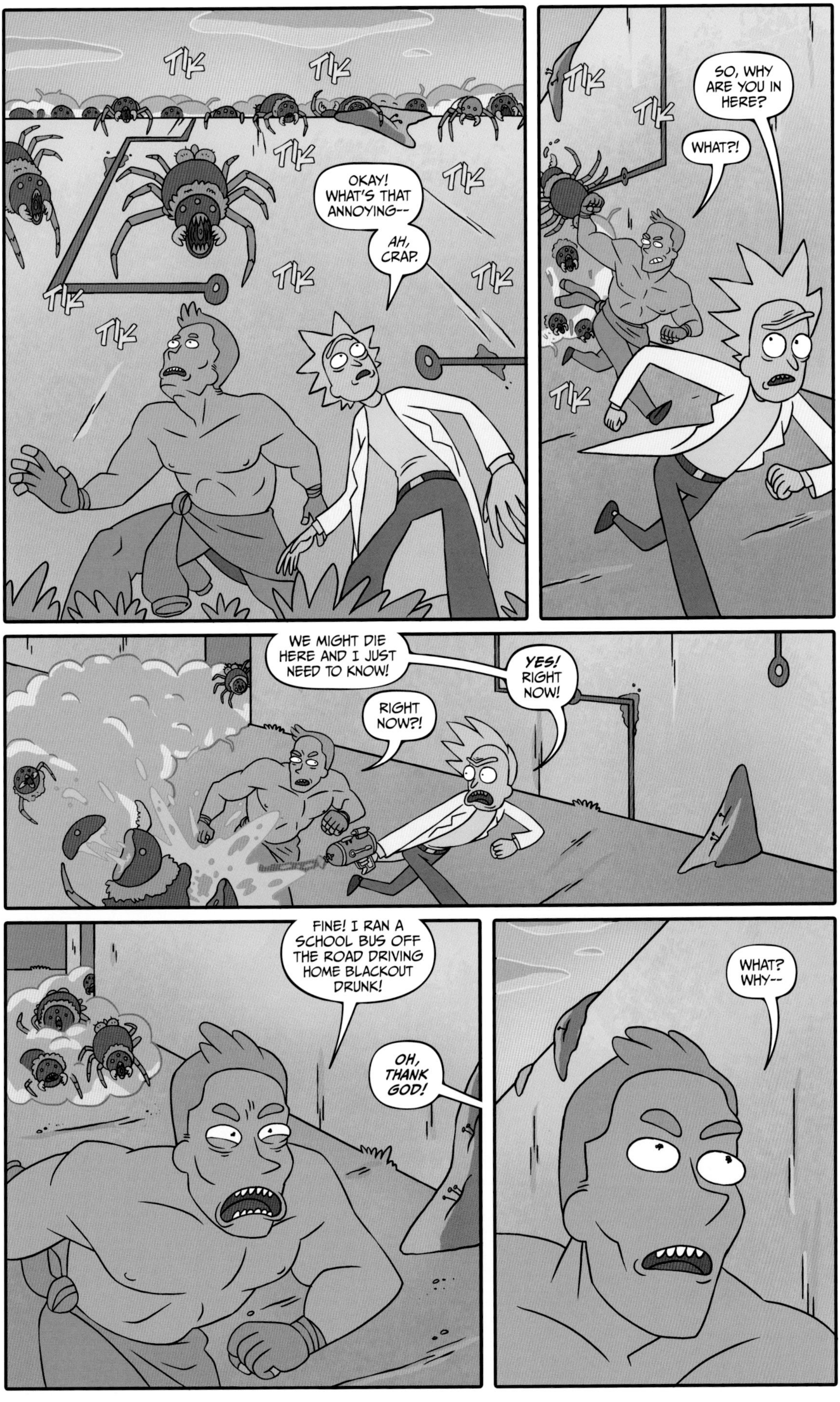
TIK
TIK
TIK
TIK
OKAY! WHAT'S THAT ANNOYING--
AH, CRAP.
TIK
TIK
SO, WHY ARE YOU IN HERE?
WHAT?!
WE MIGHT DIE HERE AND I JUST NEED TO KNOW!
RIGHT NOW?!
YES! RIGHT NOW!
FINE! I RAN A SCHOOL BUS OFF THE ROAD DRIVING HOME BLACKOUT DRUNK!
OH, THANK GOD!
WHAT? WHY--

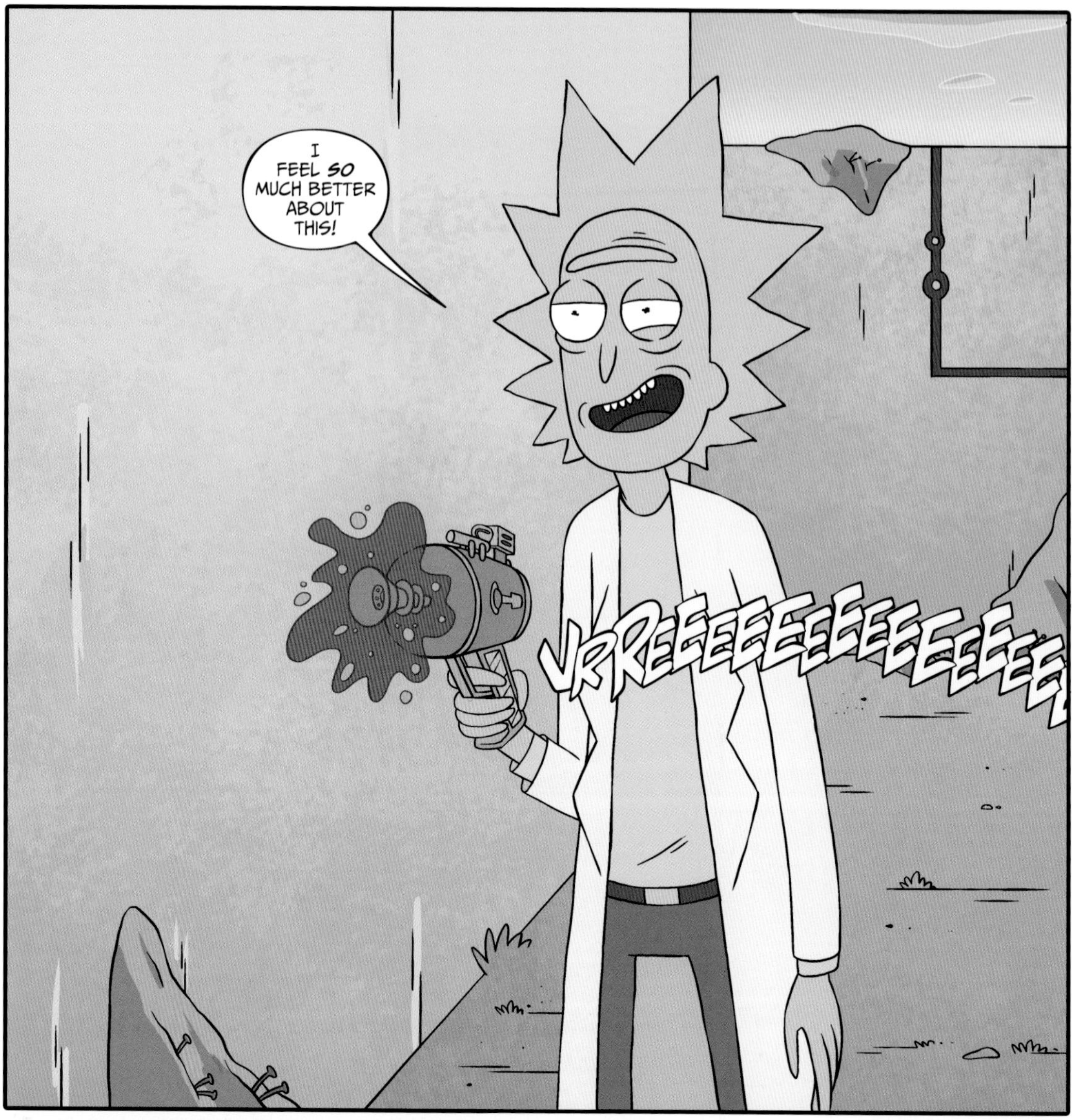
I FEEL SO MUCH BETTER ABOUT THIS!
VRREEEEEEEEEEEEEE

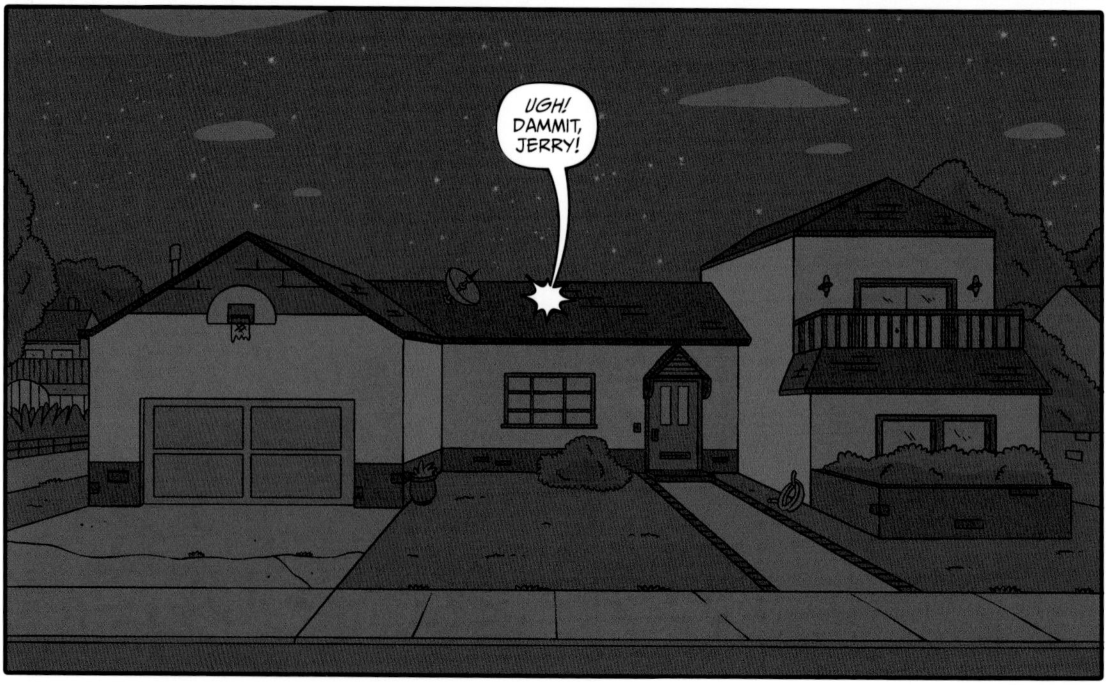
UGH! DAMMIT, JERRY!

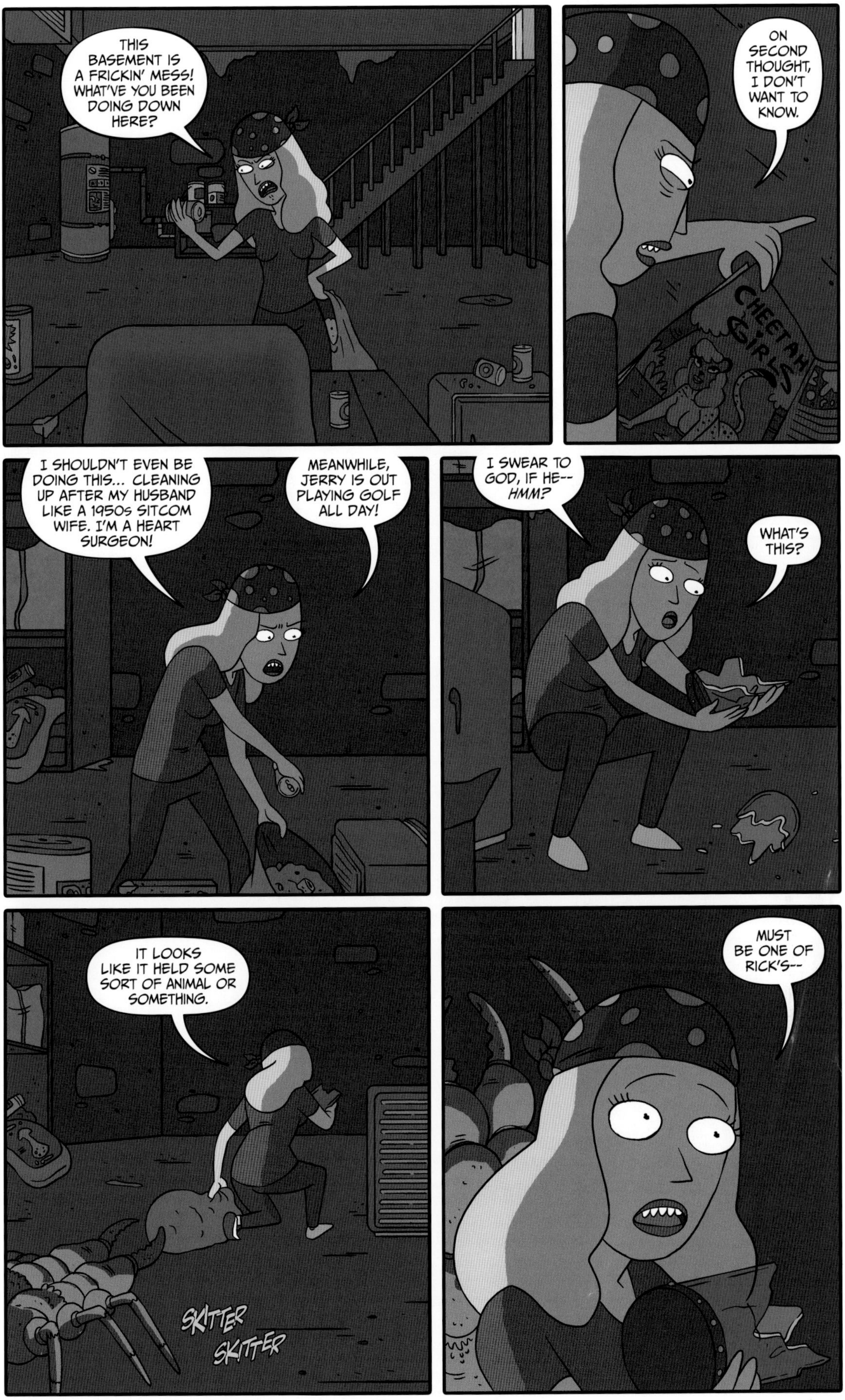
THIS BASEMENT IS A FRICKIN' MESS! WHAT'VE YOU BEEN DOING DOWN HERE?
ON SECOND THOUGHT, I DON'T WANT TO KNOW.
CHEETAH GIRLS
I SHOULDN'T EVEN BE DOING THIS... CLEANING UP AFTER MY HUSBAND LIKE A 1950s SITCOM WIFE. I'M A HEART SURGEON!
MEANWHILE, JERRY IS OUT PLAYING GOLF ALL DAY!
I SWEAR TO GOD, IF HE-- *HMM?*
WHAT'S THIS?
IT LOOKS LIKE IT HELD SOME SORT OF ANIMAL OR SOMETHING.
SKITTER
SKITTER
MUST BE ONE OF RICK'S--

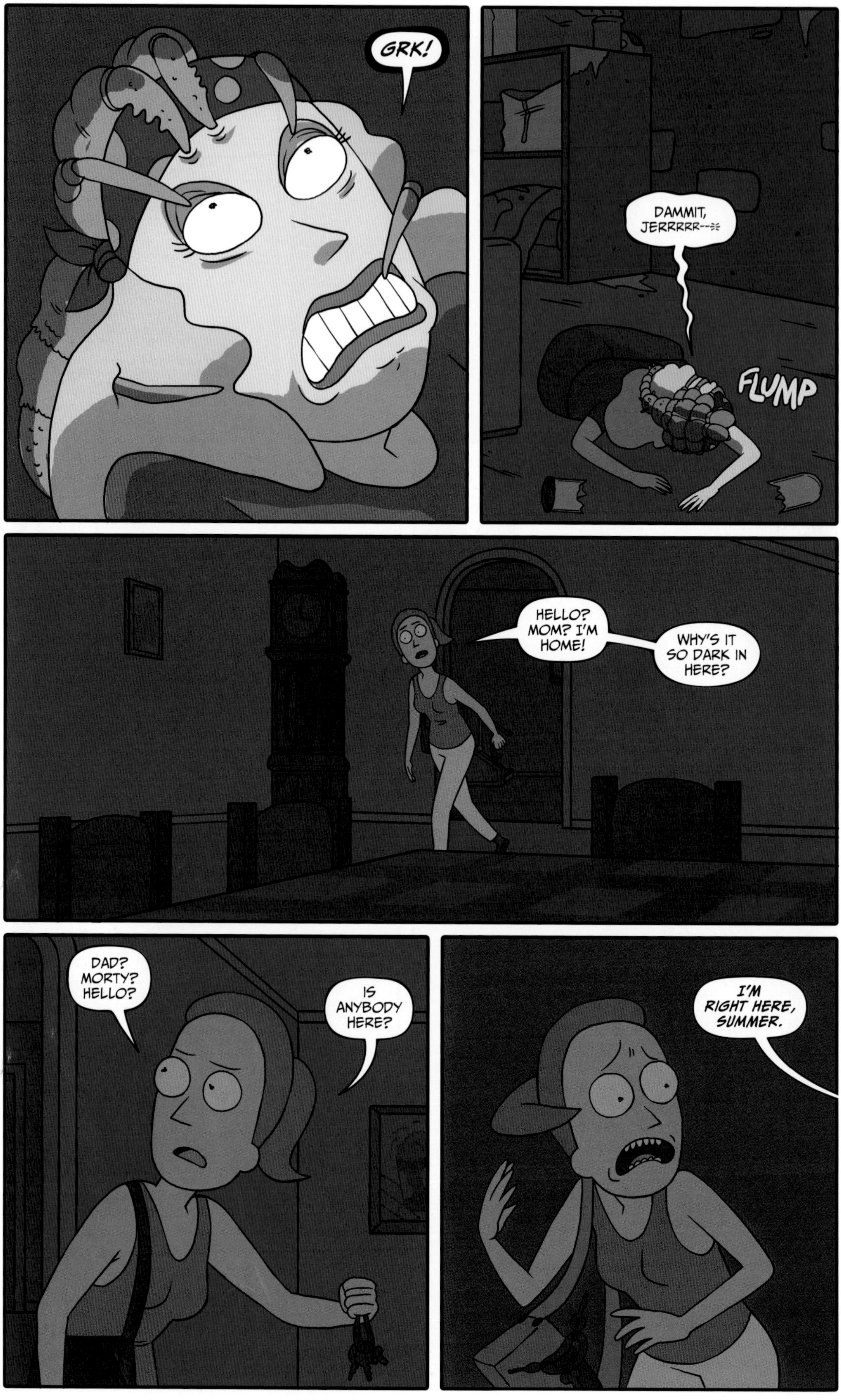
GRK!
DAMMIT, JERRRRR--
FLUMP
HELLO? MOM? I'M HOME!
WHY'S IT SO DARK IN HERE?
DAD? MORTY? HELLO?
IS ANYBODY HERE?
I'M RIGHT HERE, SUMMER.

55

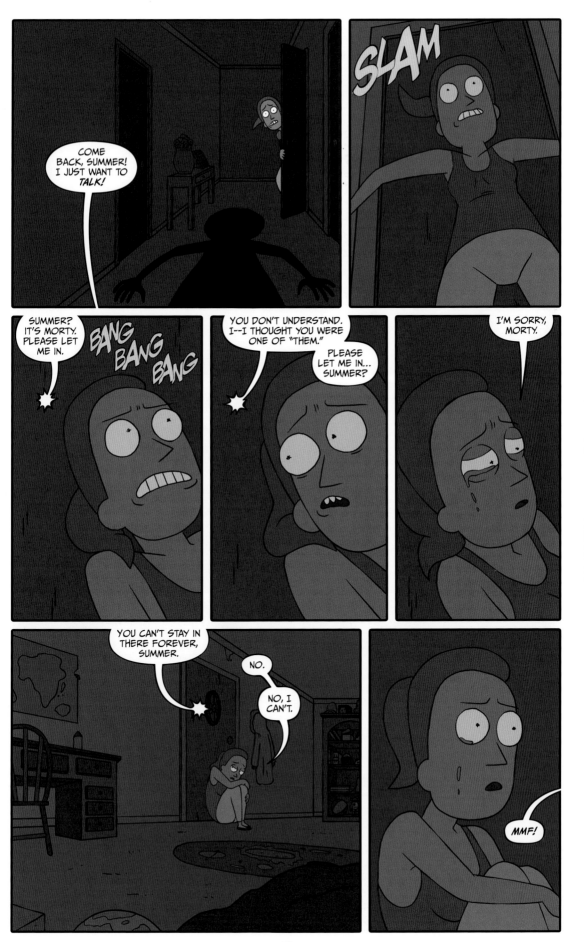

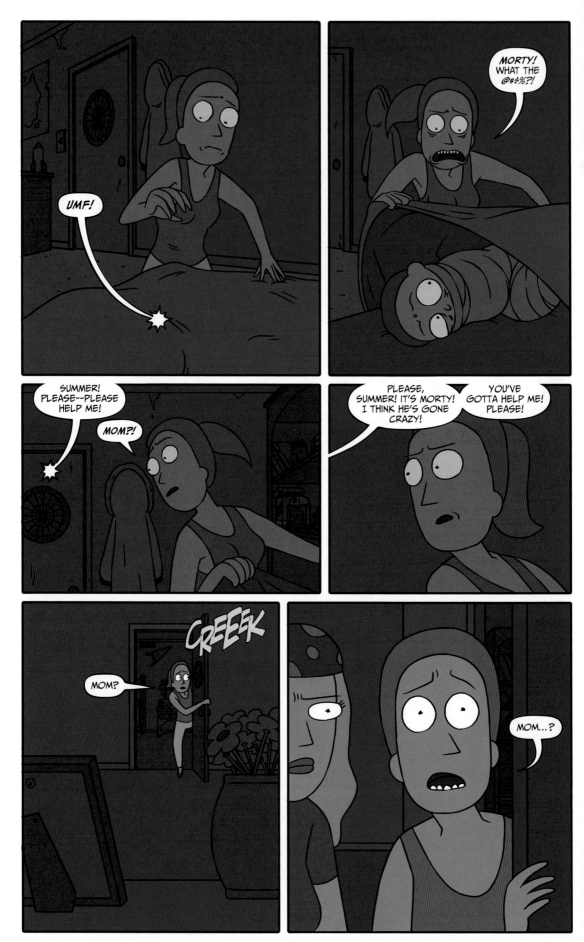

58

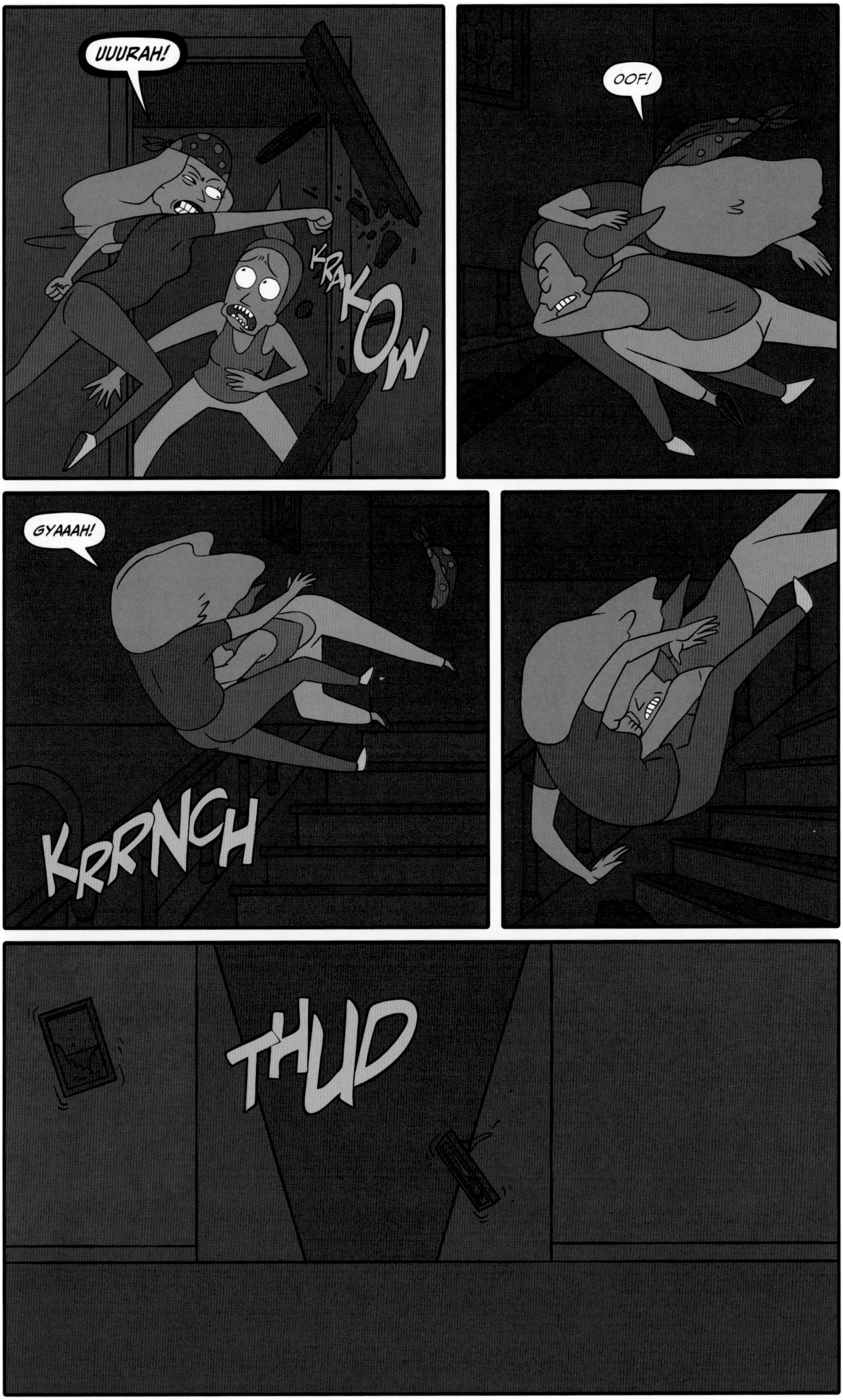
UUURAH!
KRAKOW
OOF!
GYAAAH!
KRRNCH
THUD

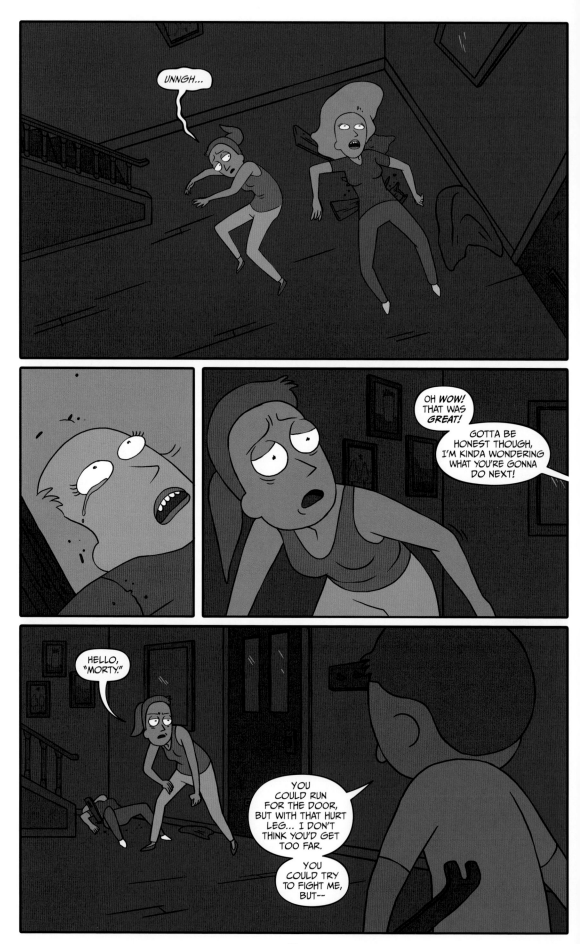

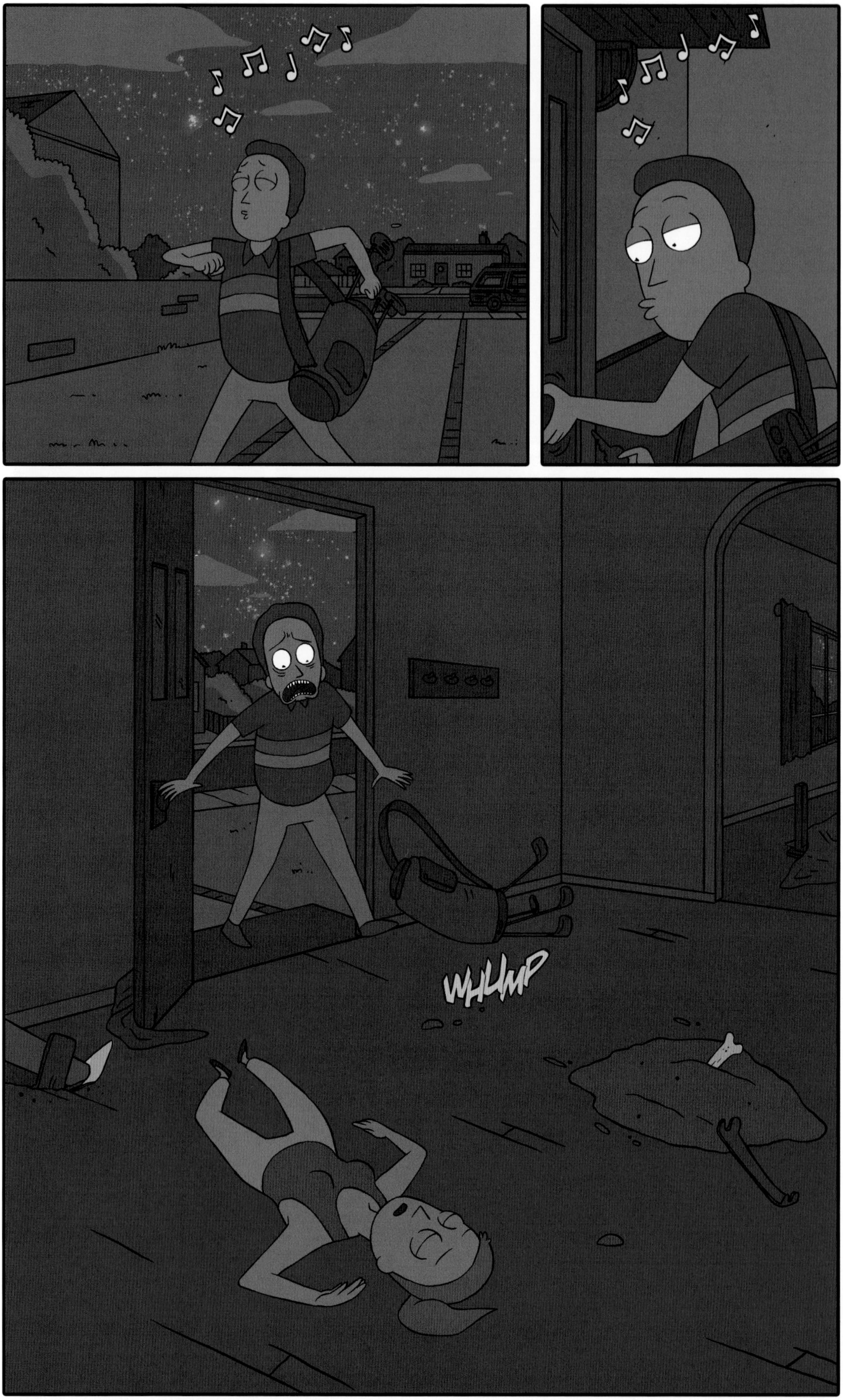
WHUMP

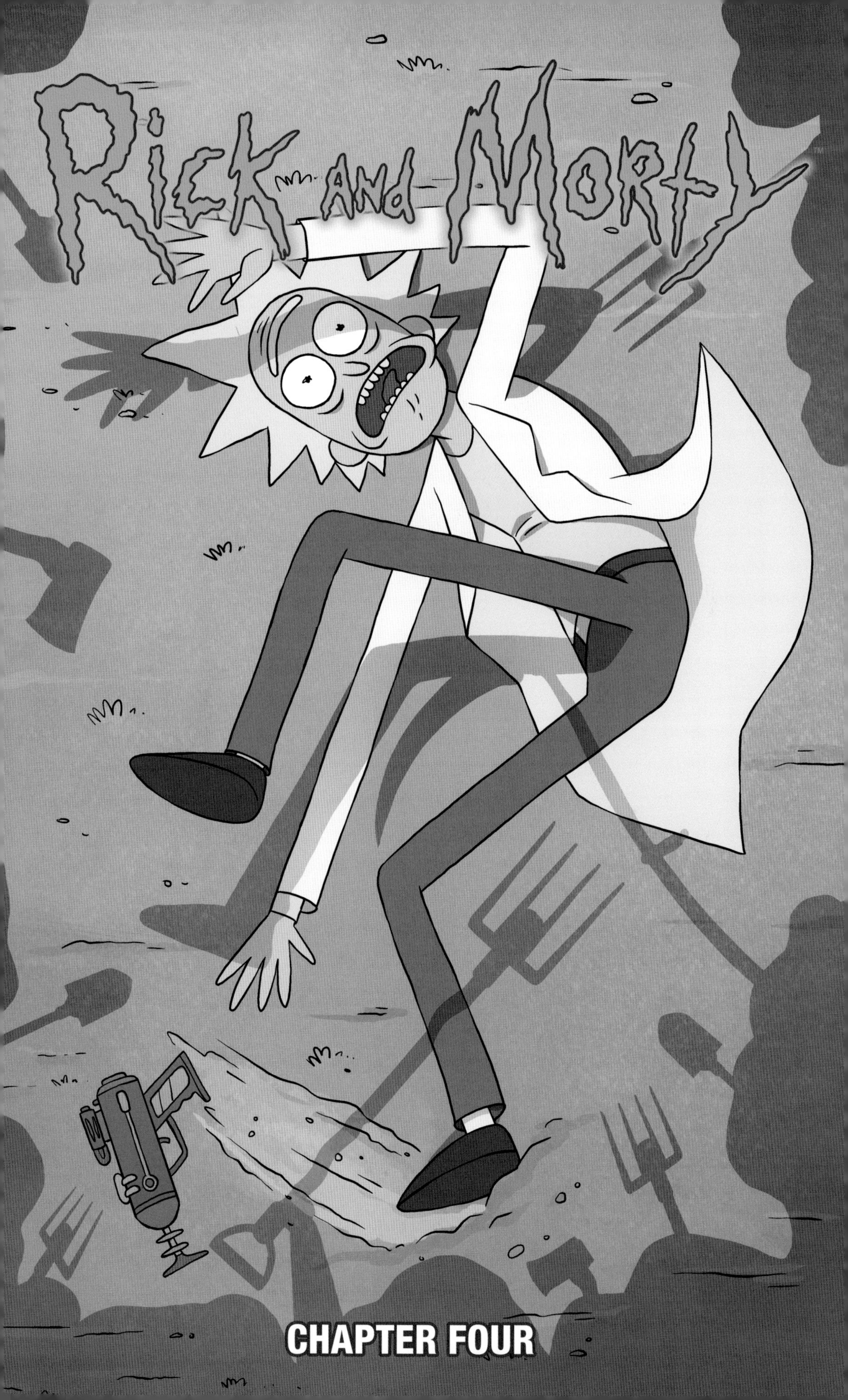
Rick and Morty

CHAPTER FOUR

69

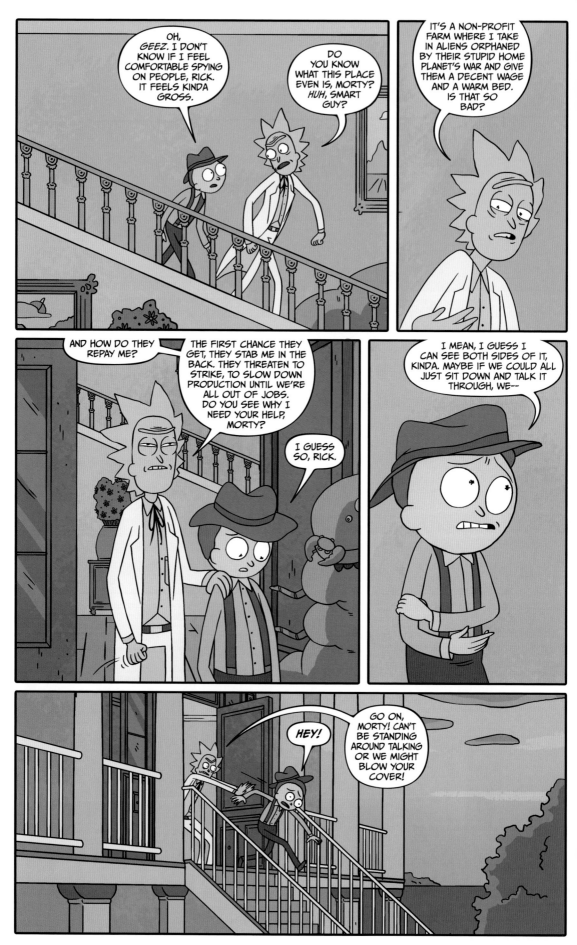

70

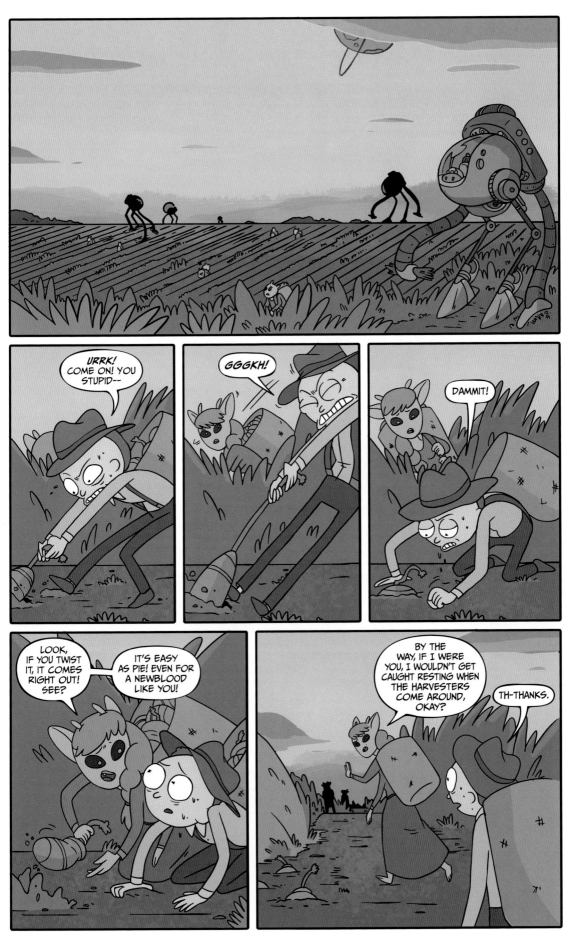

72

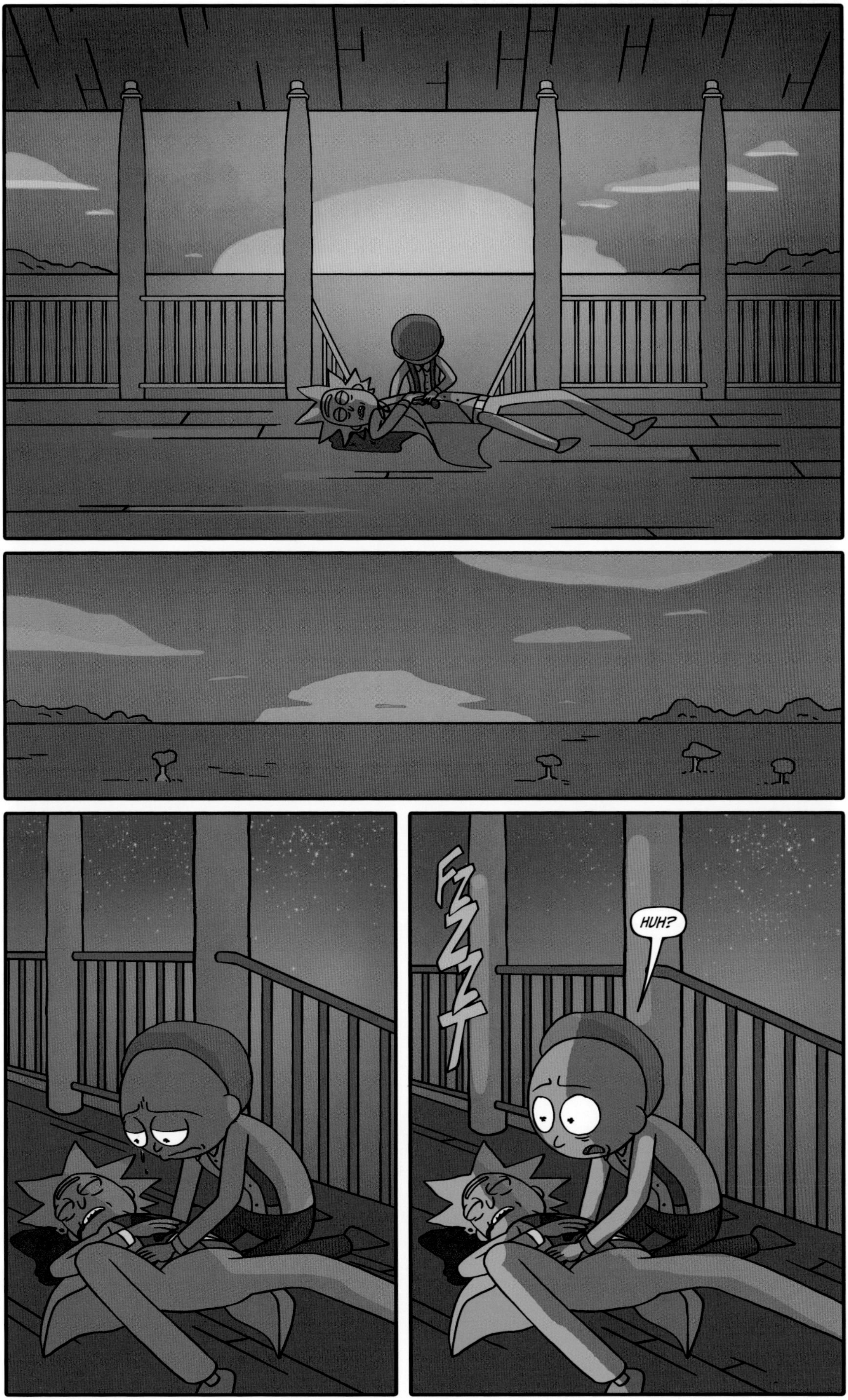
FZZZT
HUH?

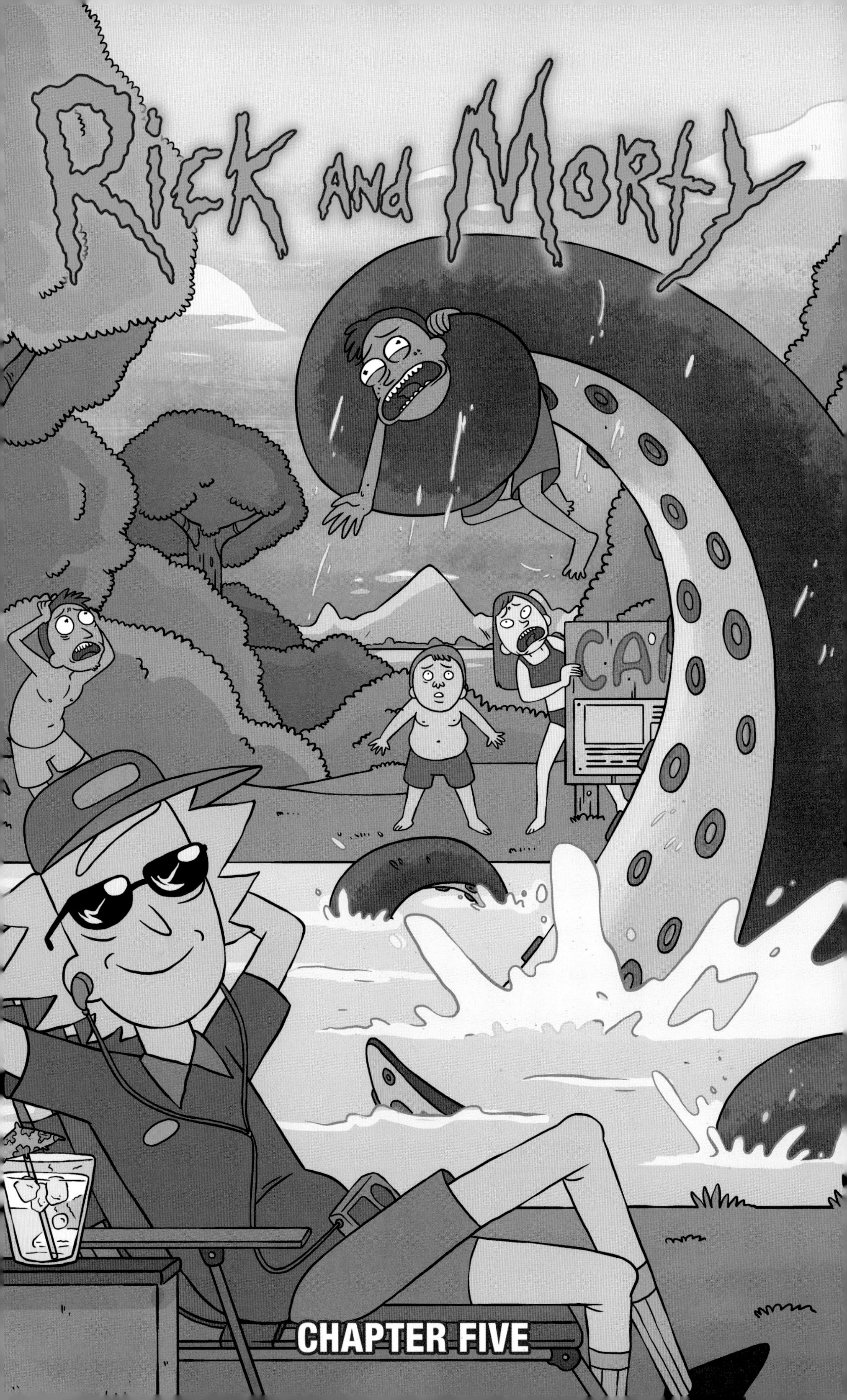
Rick and Morty™

CHAPTER FIVE

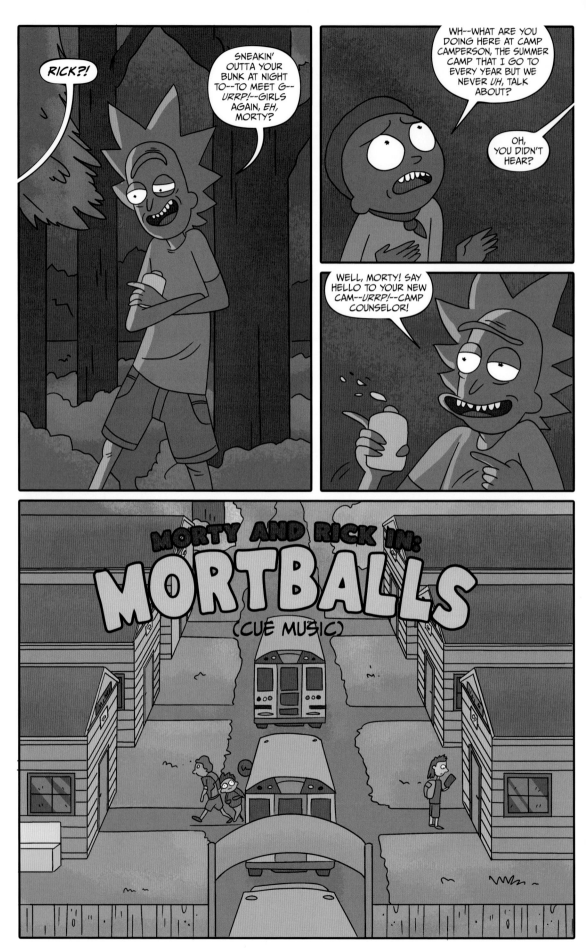

90

95

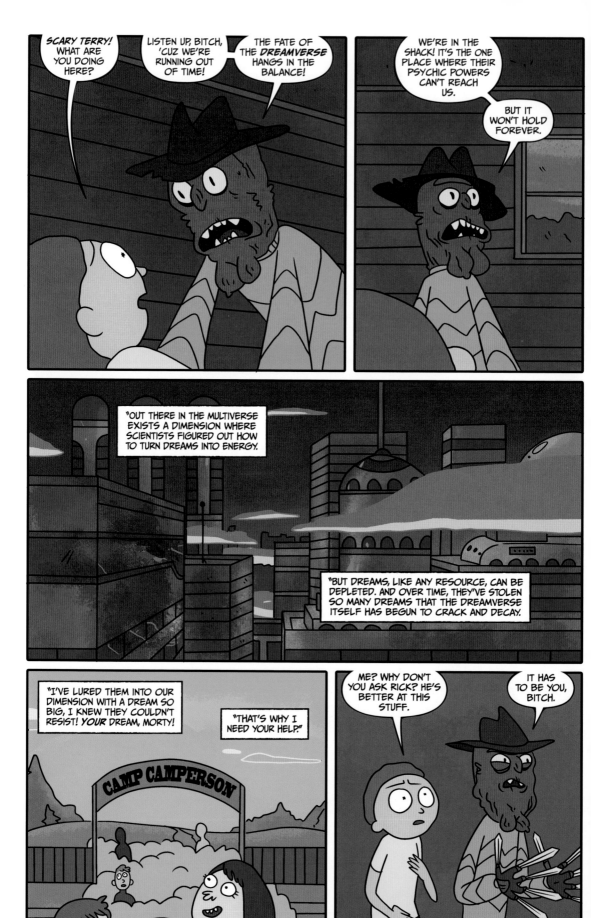

SCARY TERRY! WHAT ARE YOU DOING HERE?

LISTEN UP, BITCH, 'CUZ WE'RE RUNNING OUT OF TIME!

THE FATE OF THE *DREAMVERSE* HANGS IN THE BALANCE!

WE'RE IN THE SHACK! IT'S THE ONE PLACE WHERE THEIR PSYCHIC POWERS CAN'T REACH US.

BUT IT WON'T HOLD FOREVER.

"OUT THERE IN THE MULTIVERSE EXISTS A DIMENSION WHERE SCIENTISTS FIGURED OUT HOW TO TURN DREAMS INTO ENERGY.

"BUT DREAMS, LIKE ANY RESOURCE, CAN BE DEPLETED. AND OVER TIME, THEY'VE STOLEN SO MANY DREAMS THAT THE DREAMVERSE ITSELF HAS BEGUN TO CRACK AND DECAY.

"I'VE LURED THEM INTO OUR DIMENSION WITH A DREAM SO BIG, I KNEW THEY COULDN'T RESIST! *YOUR* DREAM, MORTY!

"THAT'S WHY I NEED YOUR HELP."

CAMP CAMPERSON

ME? WHY DON'T YOU ASK RICK? HE'S BETTER AT THIS STUFF.

IT HAS TO BE YOU, BITCH.

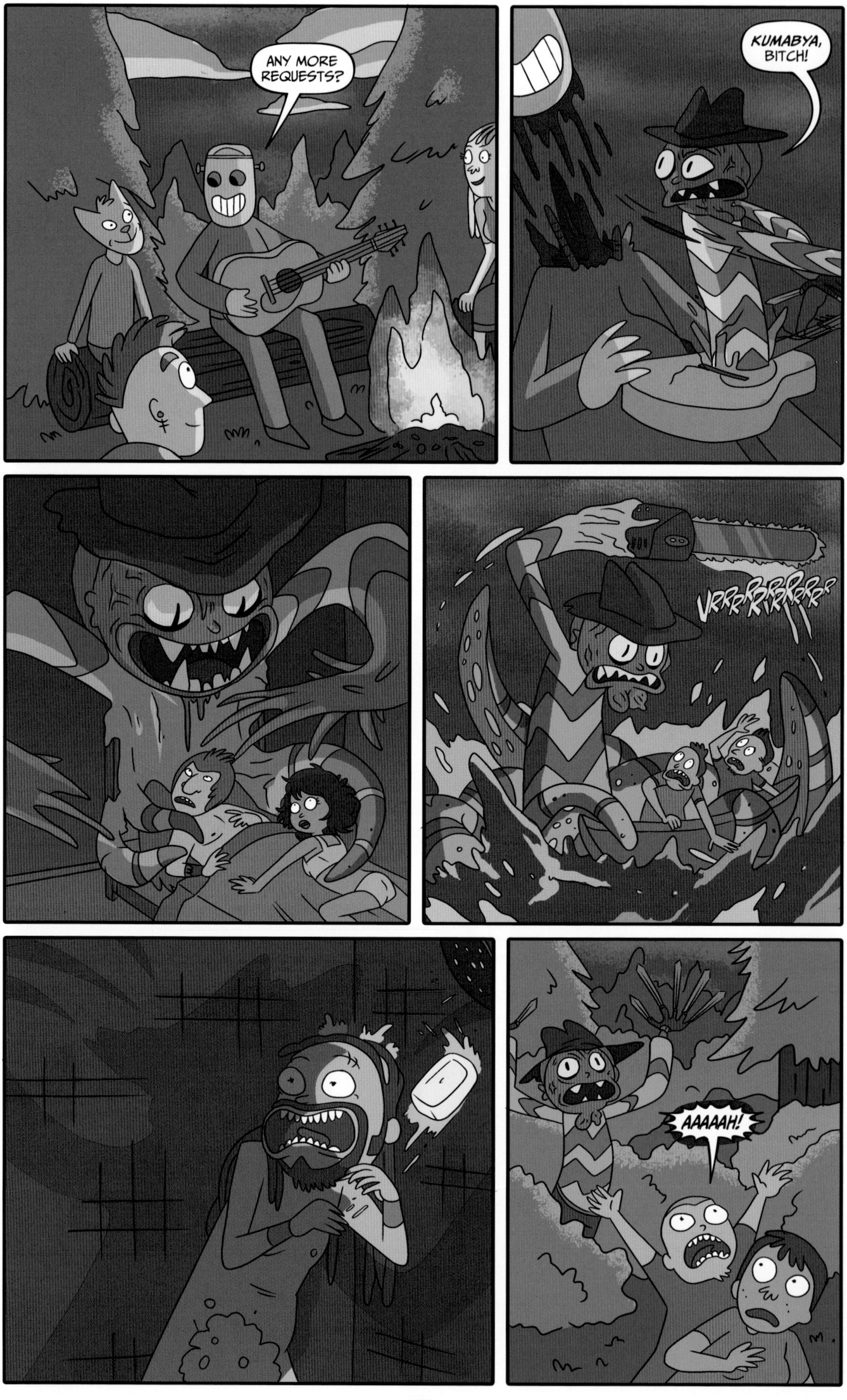
ANY MORE REQUESTS?
KUMABYA, BITCH!
VRRRRRRRRRRRR
AAAAAH!

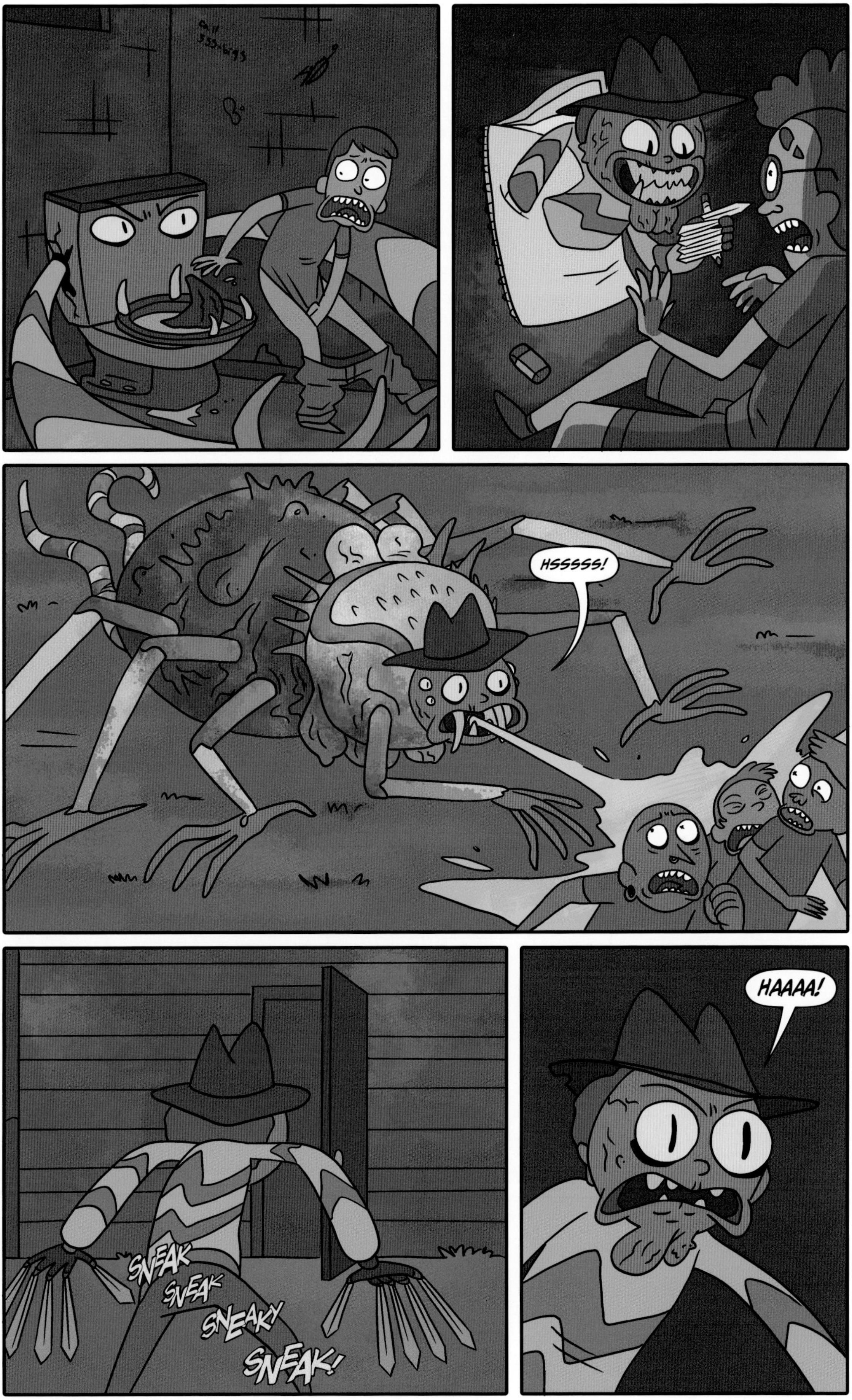
call
555-bigs
HSSSSS!
SNEAK
SNEAK
SNEAKY
SNEAK!
HAAAA!

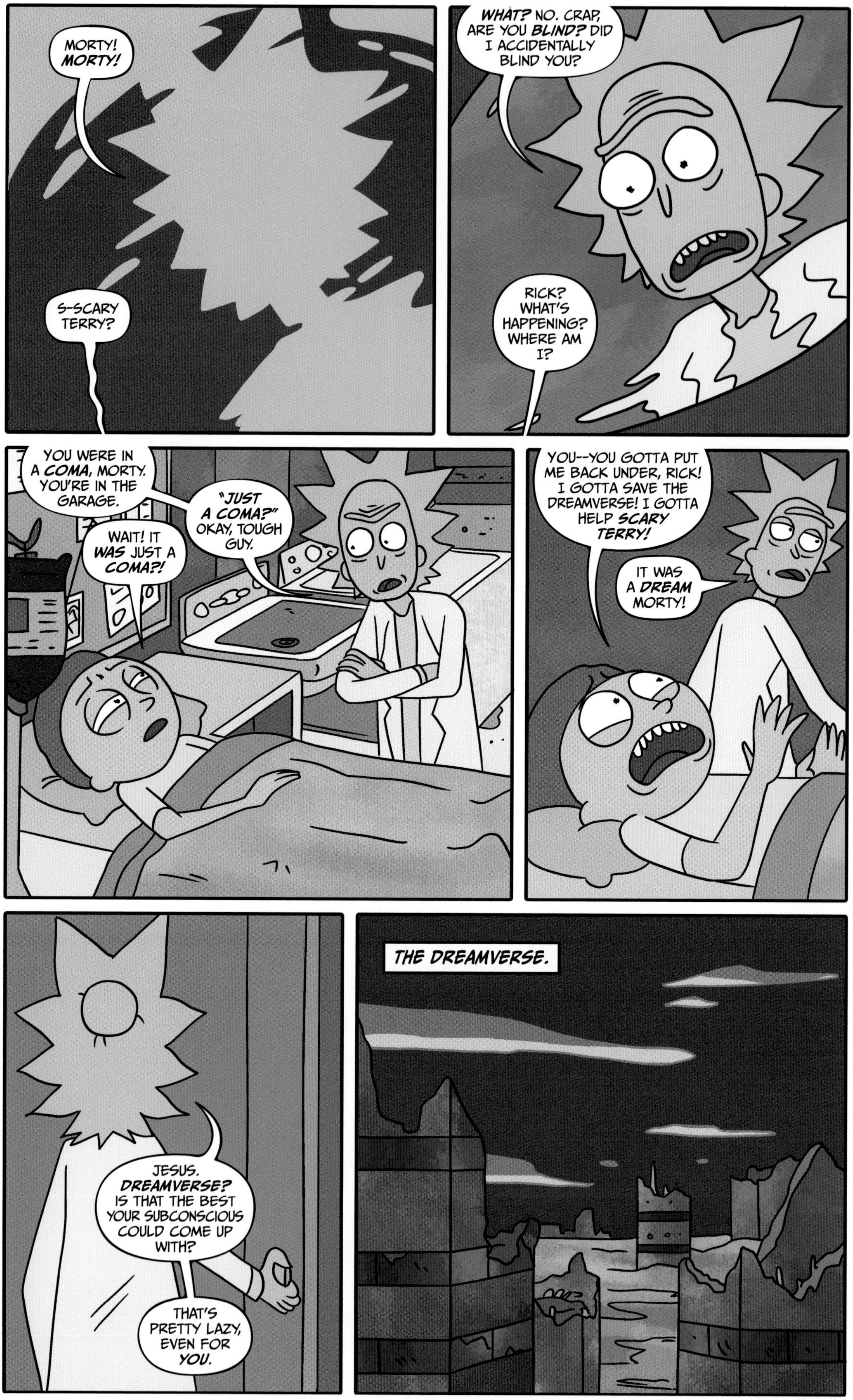
MORTY! MORTY!
S-SCARY TERRY?
WHAT? NO. CRAP, ARE YOU BLIND? DID I ACCIDENTALLY BLIND YOU?
RICK? WHAT'S HAPPENING? WHERE AM I?
YOU WERE IN A COMA, MORTY. YOU'RE IN THE GARAGE.
WAIT! IT WAS JUST A COMA?!
"JUST A COMA?" OKAY, TOUGH GUY.
YOU--YOU GOTTA PUT ME BACK UNDER, RICK! I GOTTA SAVE THE DREAMVERSE! I GOTTA HELP SCARY TERRY!
IT WAS A DREAM MORTY!
JESUS. DREAMVERSE? IS THAT THE BEST YOUR SUBCONSCIOUS COULD COME UP WITH?
THAT'S PRETTY LAZY, EVEN FOR YOU.
THE DREAMVERSE.

BONUS SHORTS

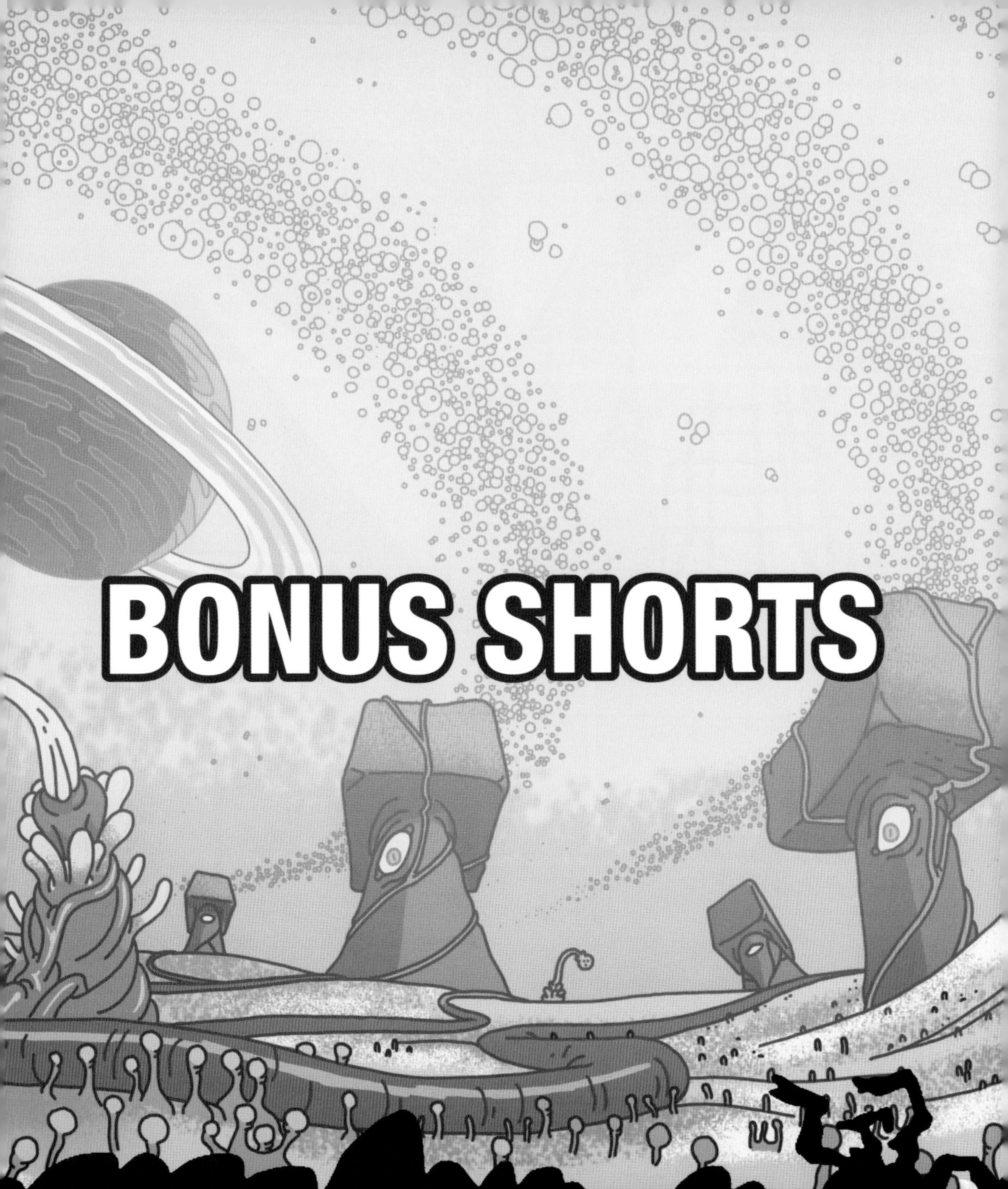

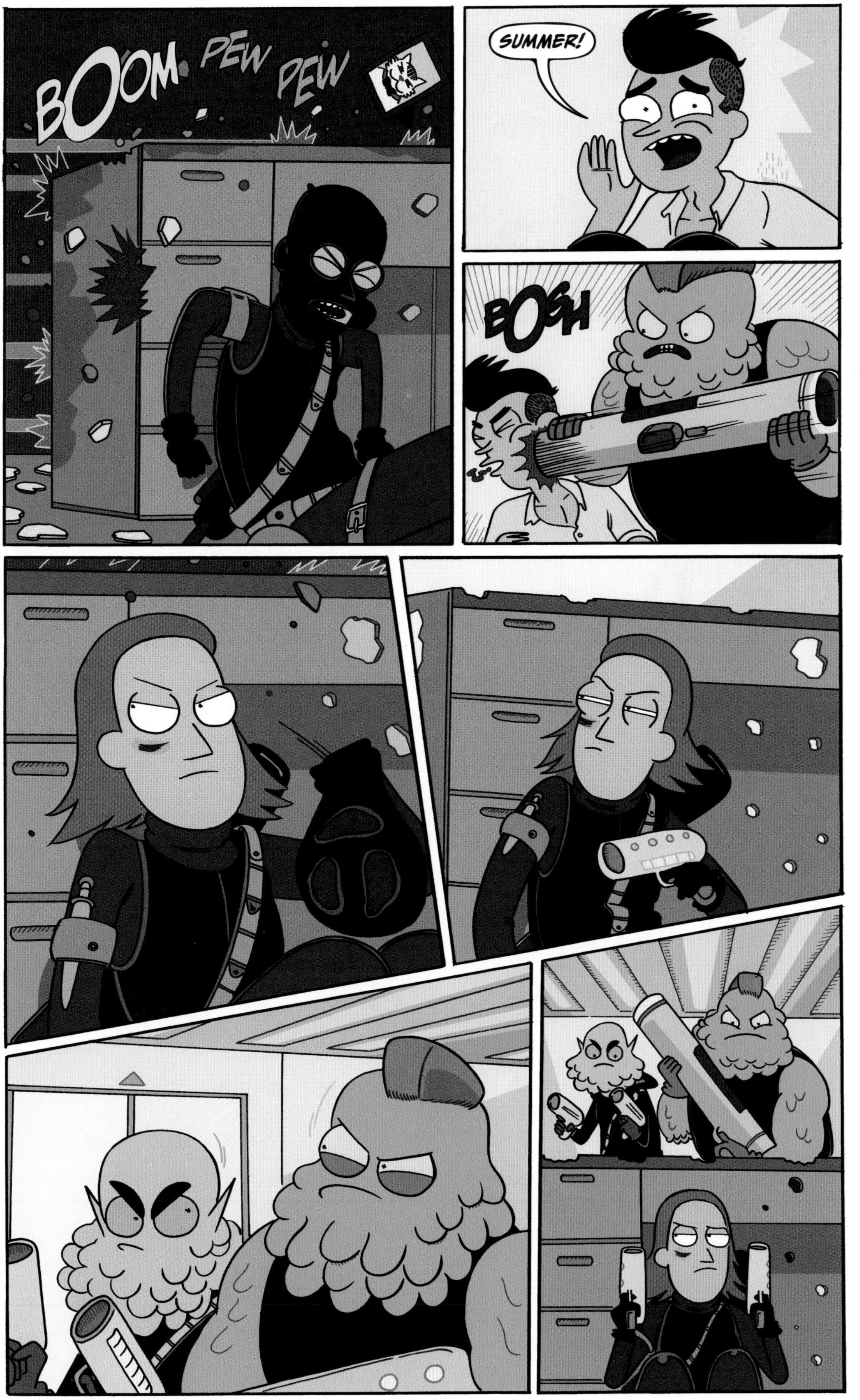
BOOM PEW PEW
SUMMER!
BOSH

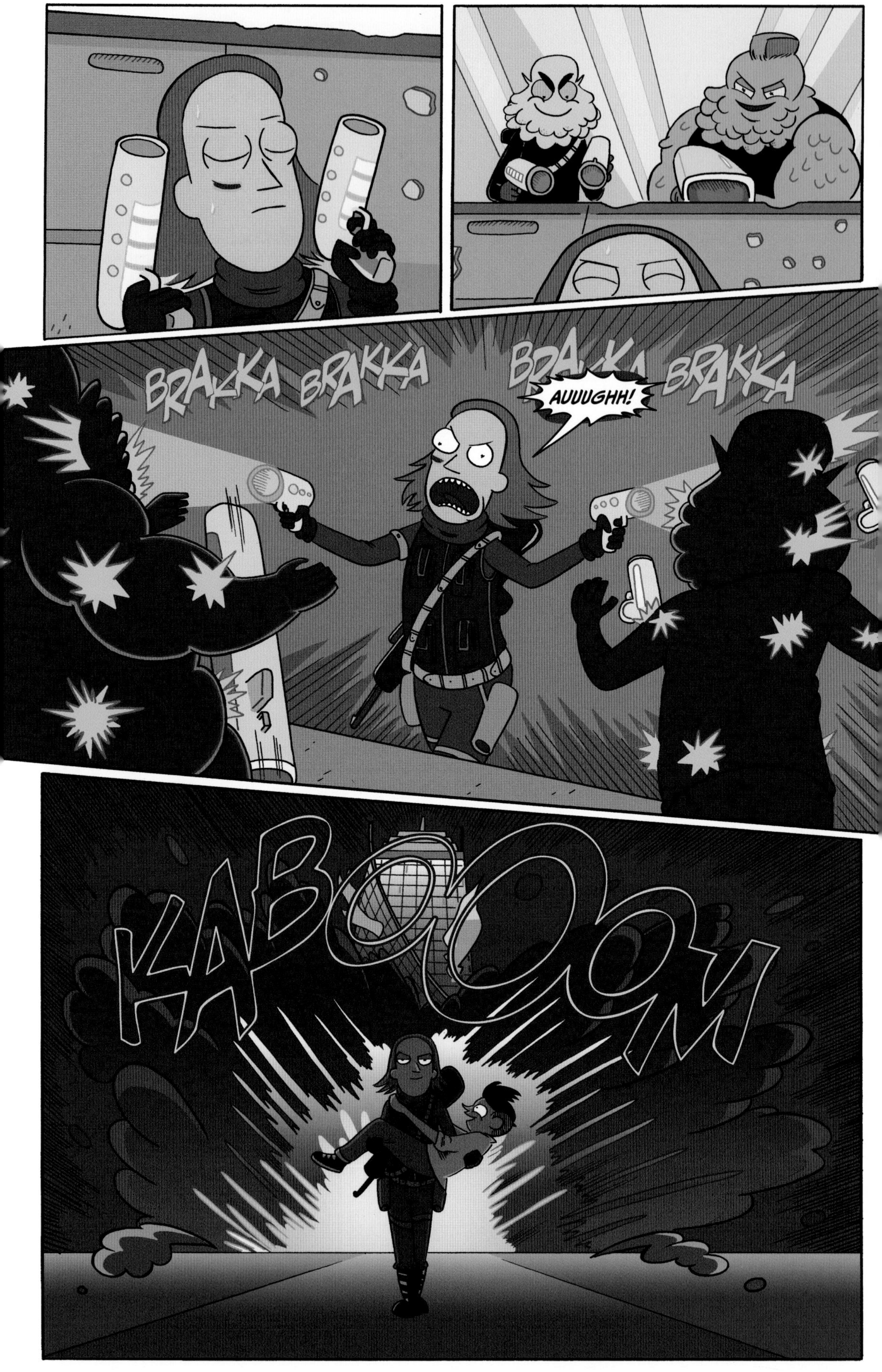
BRAKKA BRAKKA
BRAKKA BRAKKA
AUUUGHH!
KABOOOM

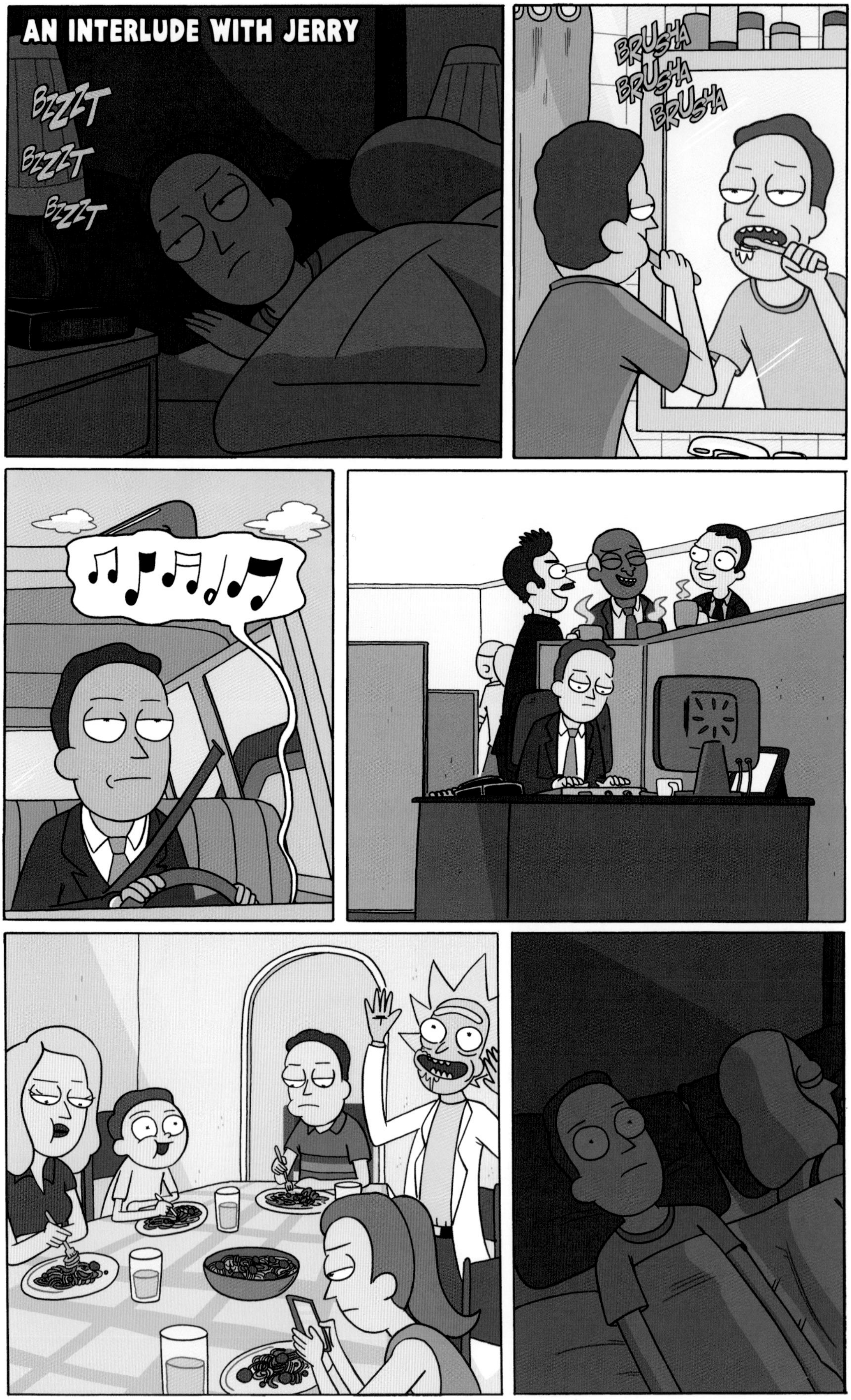
AN INTERLUDE WITH JERRY
BZZZT
BZZZT
BZZZT
BRUSHA
BRUSHA
BRUSHA

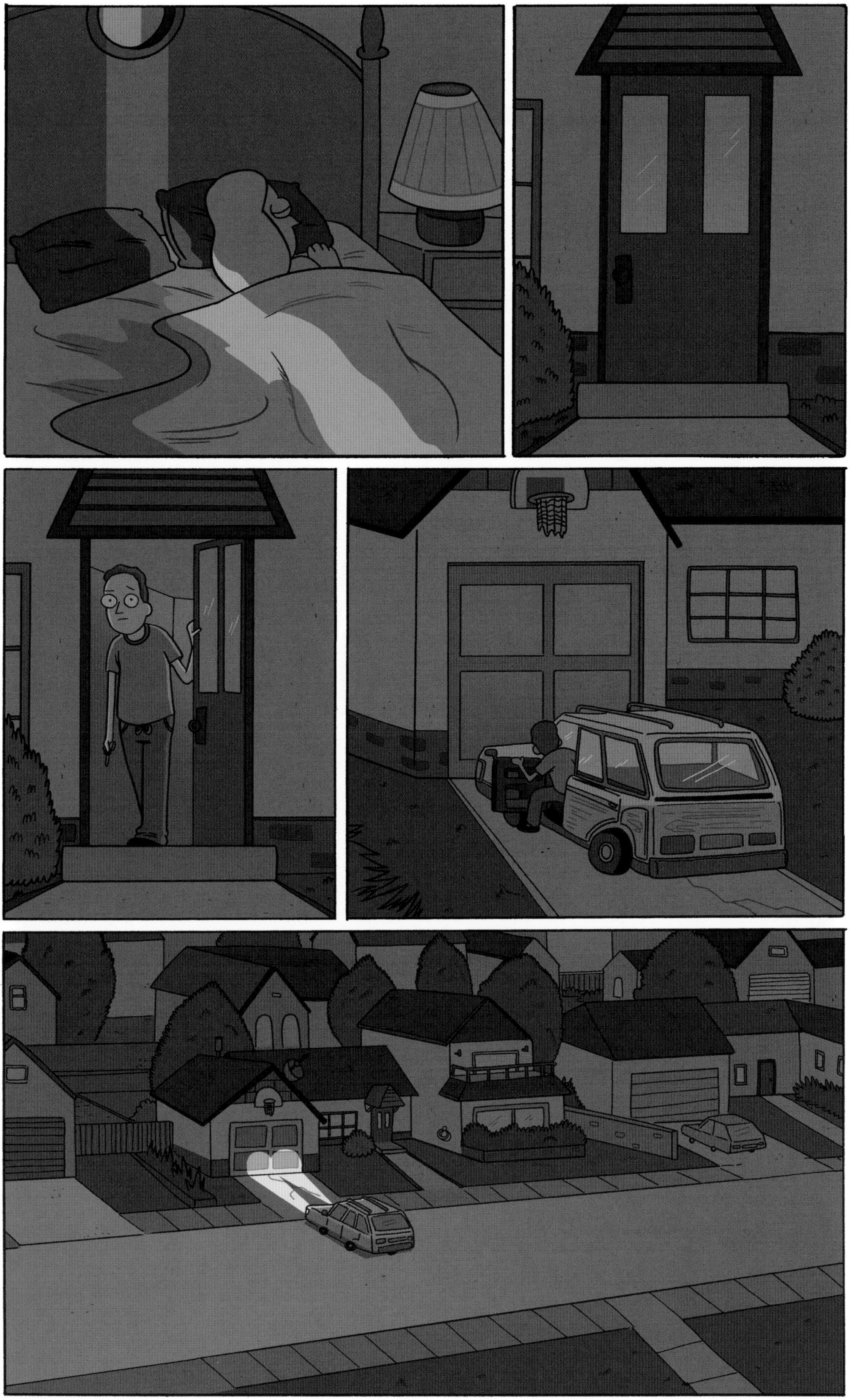

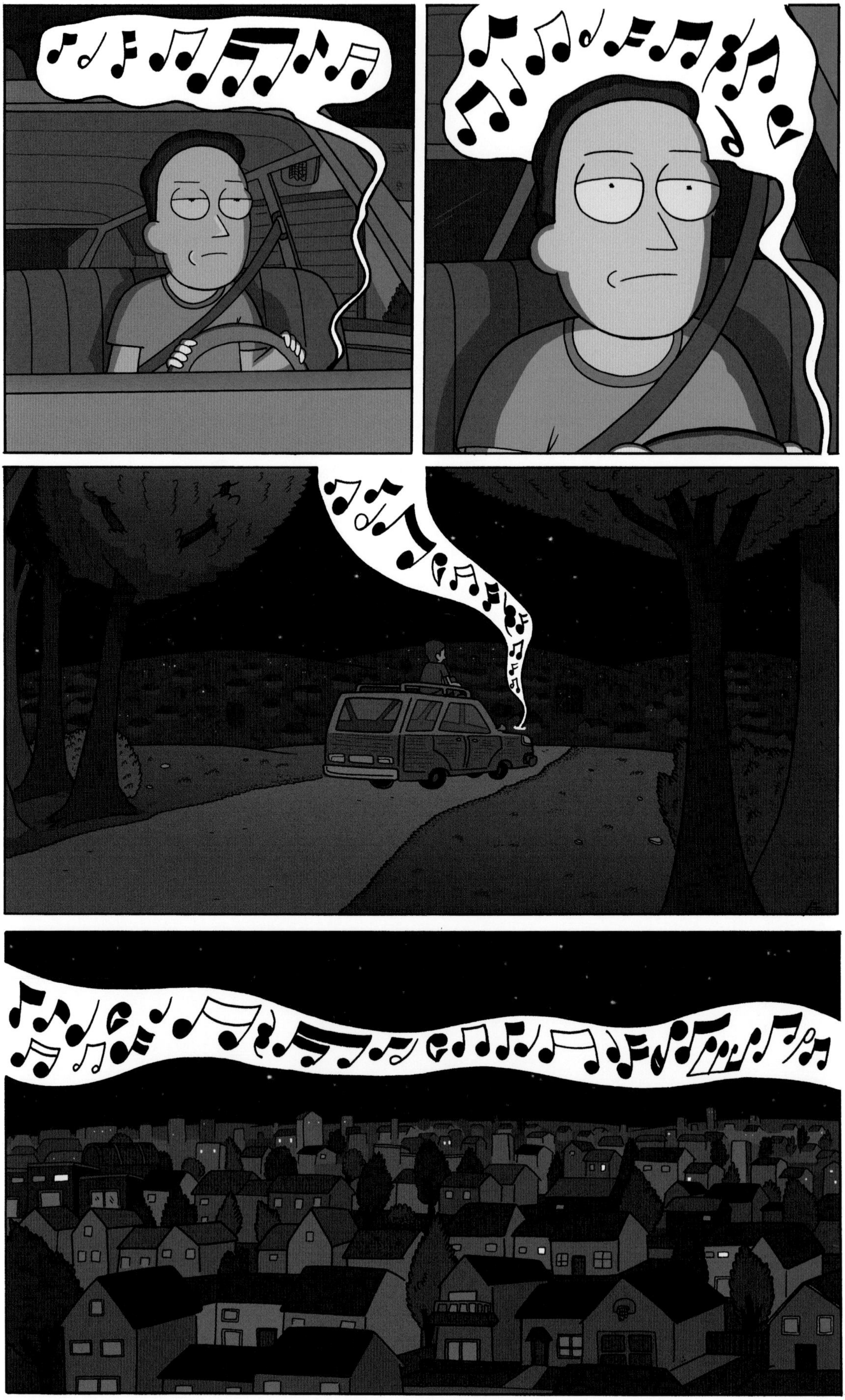

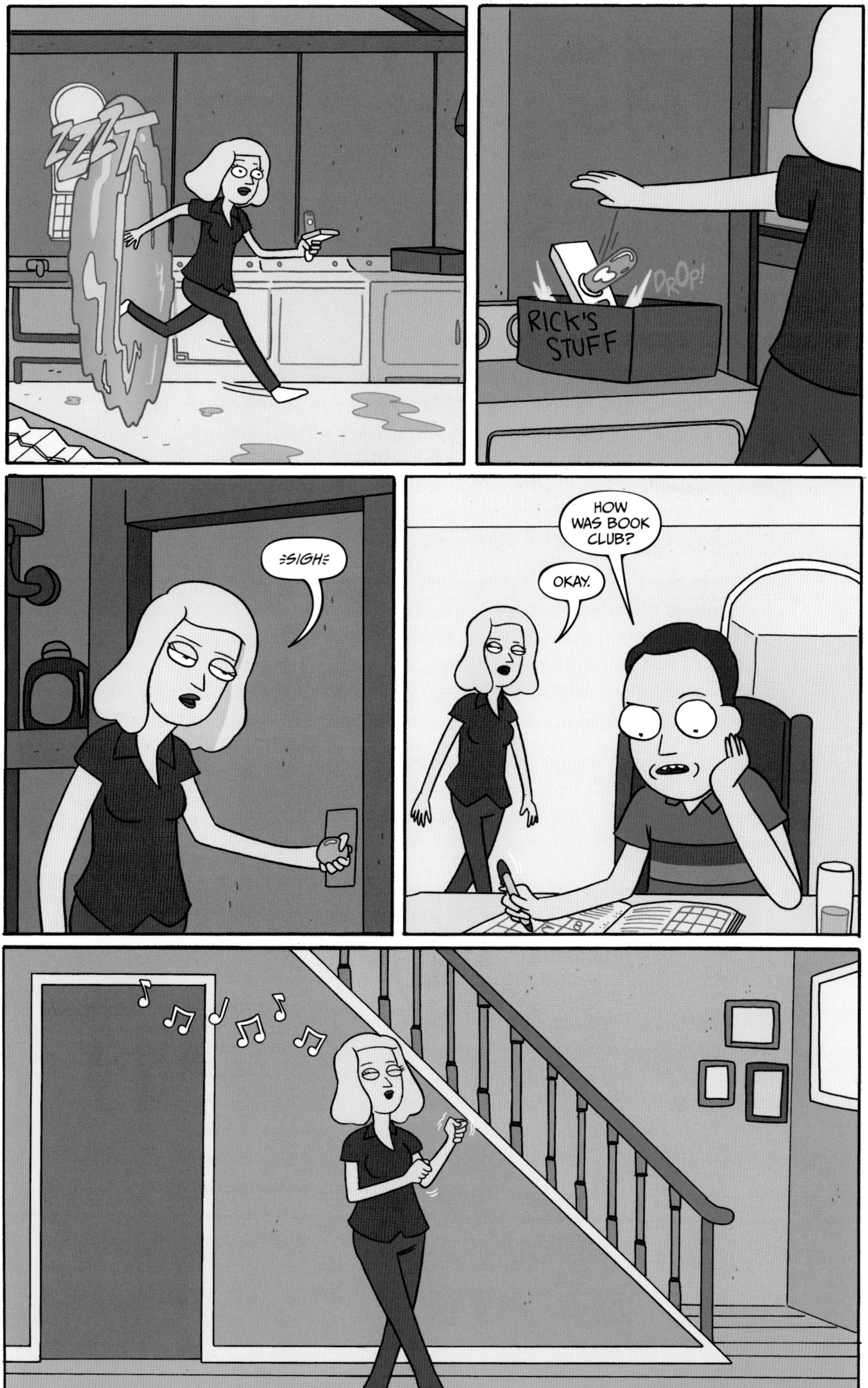
ZZZT
RICK'S STUFF
DROP!
SIGH
HOW WAS BOOK CLUB?
OKAY.
END.

DAN HARMON is the Emmy® winning creator/executive producer of the comedy series *Community* as well as the co-creator/executive producer of Adult Swim's *Rick & Morty*.

Harmon's pursuit of minimal work for maximum reward took him from stand-up to improv to sketch comedy, then finally to Los Angeles, where he began writing feature screenplays with fellow Milwaukeean Rob Schrab. As part of his deal with Robert Zemeckis at Imagemovers, Harmon co-wrote the feature film *Monster House*. Following this, Harmon co-wrote the Ben Stiller directed pilot *Heat Vision and Jack*, starring Jack Black and Owen Wilson.

Disillusioned by the legitimate industry, Harmon began attending classes at nearby Glendale Community College. At the same time, Harmon and Schrab founded Channel 101, an untelevised non-profit audience-controlled network for undiscovered filmmakers, many of whom used it to launch mainstream careers, including the boys behind SNL's Digital Shorts. Harmon, along with Schrab, partnered with Sarah Silverman to create her Comedy Central series, *The Sarah Silverman Program*, where he served as head writer for the first season.

Harmon went on to create, write and perform in the short-lived VH1 sketch series *Acceptable TV* before eventually creating the critically acclaimed and fan favorite comedy *Community*. The show originally aired on NBC for five seasons before being acquired by Yahoo which premiered season six of the show in March of 2015. In 2009 he won an Emmy for Outstanding Music and Lyrics for the opening number of the 81st Annual Academy Awards.

Along with Justin Roiland, Harmon created the breakout Adult Swim animated series *Rick & Morty*. The show premiered in December of 2013 and quickly became a ratings hit. Harmon and Roiland have wrapped up season two, which premiered in 2015.

In 2014 Harmon was the star of the documentary *Harmontown* which premiered at the SXSW Film Festival and chronicled his 20-city stand-up/podcast tour of the same name. The documentary was released theatrically in October of 2014.

——

JUSTIN ROILAND grew up in Manteca, California where he did the basic stuff children do. Later in life he traveled to Los Angeles. Once settled in, he created several popular online shorts for Channel101. Some notable examples of his work (both animated and live action) include *House of Cosbys* and *Two Girls One Cup: The Show*. Justin is afraid of his mortality and hopes the things he creates will make lots of people happy. Then maybe when modern civilization collapses into chaos, people will remember him and they'll help him survive the bloodshed and violence. Global economic collapse is looming. It's going to be horrible, and honestly, a swift death might be preferable than living in the hell that awaits mankind. Justin also really hates writing about himself in the third person. I hate this. That's right. It's me. I've been writing this whole thing. Hi. The cat's out of the bag. It's just you and me now. There never was a third person. If you want to know anything about me, just ask. Sorry this wasn't more informative.

ZAC GORMAN is an Eisner Award-wanting cartoonist and writer from Detroit, Michigan, best known for his work on beating Super Mario Bros. 2 without the use of a Game Genie. Outside comics, he frequently works in television animation, doing storyboards and character designs for several hit shows with highly financially lucrative target demographics.

CJ CANNON is primarily a "stripper" and self-taught artist living in Nashville, Tennessee. When they're not working on comics, outside riding their bike, or drumming, they're almost always in the house drawing gross fanart and fandom smut for similarly gross people. CJ has: two cats, three hermit crabs, a hamster, an eldritch abomination, a pacman frog, and a leopard gecko.

RYAN HILL has colored some comics so far. Many of these include *Stumptown*, *Judge Dredd Mega City 2*, *Age of Reptiles*, *Terrible Lizard*, *Sixth Gun: Valley of Death*, *Avatar The Last Airbender*, and *EGO*. The pizza guy who delivers his lunch every "ZA & Wing Wednesday" is rumored to have once said, "Not bad, man" in regard to the work.

MARC ELLERBY is a comics illustrator living in Essex, UK. He has worked on such titles as *Doctor Who*, *Regular Show*, and *The Amazing World of Gumball*. His own comics (which you should totally check out!) are *Chloe Noonan: Monster Hunter*, and *Ellerbisms*. You can read some comics if you like at marcellerby.com.

CHRIS CRANK has worked on several recent Oni Press books like *The Sixth Gun*, *Brides of Helheim*, *Terrible Lizard*, and others. Or maybe you've seen his letters in *Revival*, *Hack/Slash*, *God Hates Astronauts*, or *Dark Engine* from Image. Or perhaps you've read *Lady Killer* or *Sundowners* from Dark Horse. Heck, you might even be reading the award winning *Battlepug* at battlepug.com right now!

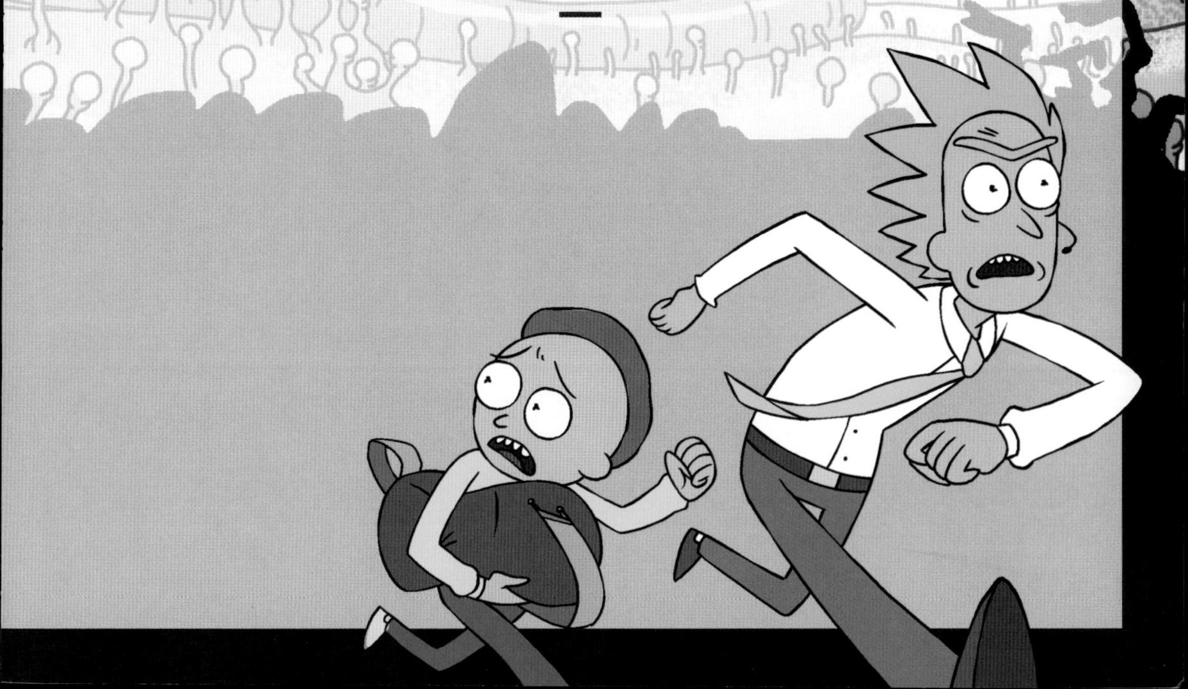

MORE BOOKS FROM ONI PRESS

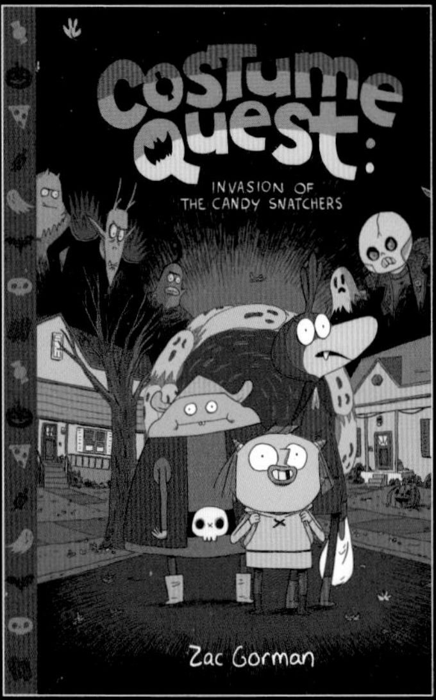
Costume Quest:
INVASION OF THE CANDY SNATCHERS
Zac Gorman

COSTUME QUEST: INVASION OF THE CANDY SNATCHERS
By Zac Gorman
56 pages, hardcover, color
ISBN 978-1-62010-190-2

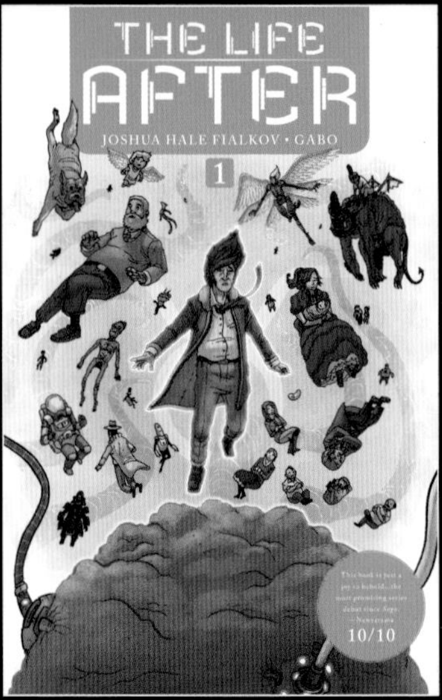
THE LIFE AFTER
JOSHUA HALE FIALKOV • GABO
1
10/10

THE LIFE AFTER, VOLUME ONE
By Joshua Hale Fialkov and Gabo
136 pages, softcover, color
ISBN 978-1-62010-214-5

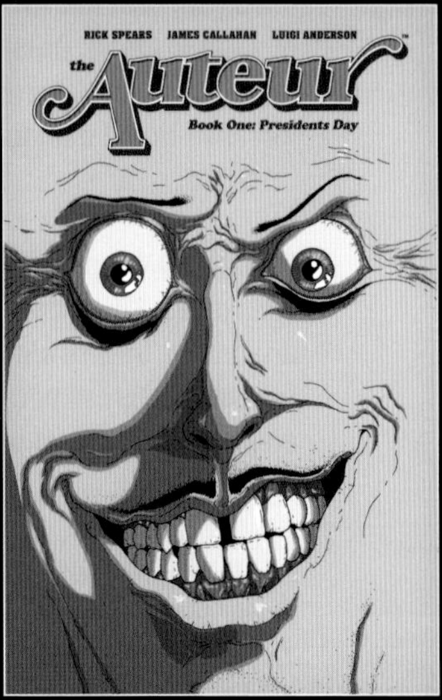
RICK SPEARS JAMES CALLAHAN LUIGI ANDERSON
the Auteur
Book One: Presidents Day

THE AUTEUR, BOOK ONE: PRESIDENTS DAY
By Rick Spears & James Callahan
144 pages, softcover, color
ISBN 978-1-62010-135-3

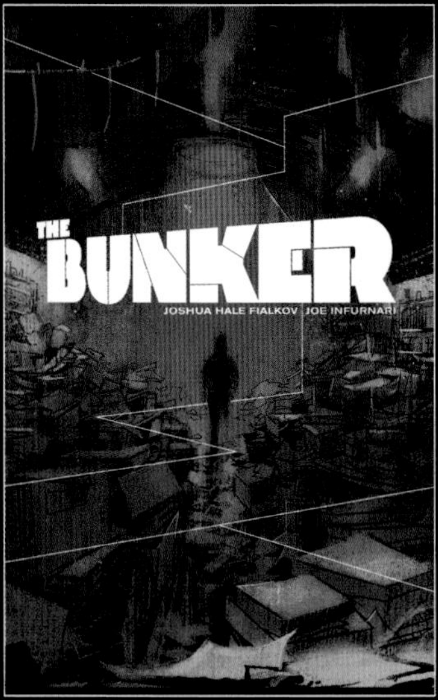
THE BUNKER
JOSHUA HALE FIALKOV JOE INFURNARI

THE BUNKER, VOLUME 1
By Joshua Hale Fialkov & Joe Infurnari
136 pages, softcover, color
ISBN 978-1-62010-164-3

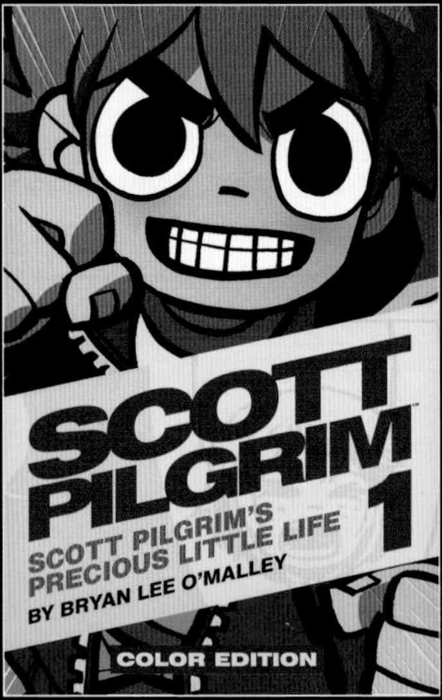
SCOTT PILGRIM 1
SCOTT PILGRIM'S PRECIOUS LITTLE LIFE
BY BRYAN LEE O'MALLEY
COLOR EDITION

SCOTT PILGRIM COLOR HARDCOVER, VOL. 1: PRECIOUS LITTLE LIFE
By Bryan Lee O'Malley
192 pages, hardcover, color
ISBN 978-1-62010-000-4

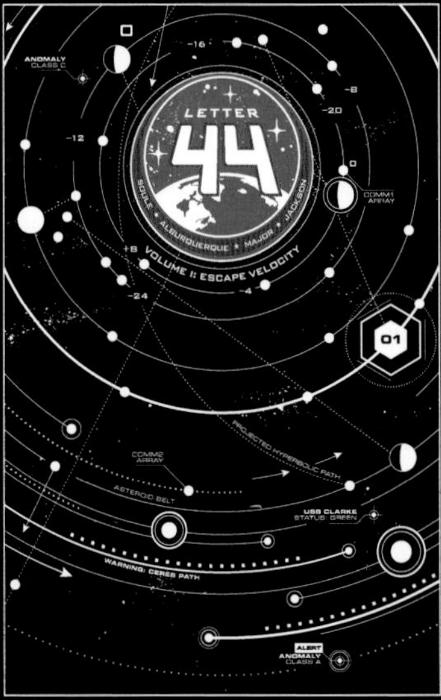
LETTER 44
SOULE ALBURQUERQUE MAJOR JACKSON
VOLUME 1: ESCAPE VELOCITY
01

LETTER 44, VOLUME 1: ESCAPE VELOCITY
By Charles Soule & Alberto Jiménez Alburquerque
160 pages, softcover, color
ISBN 978-1-62010-133-9

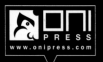